CROCHET CUTIES
Patterns for 24 Dolls and 60 Clothes and Accessories

Zess
du blog zess.fr

Stackpole Books
Guilford, Connecticut

D1261749

Published by Stackpole Books
An imprint of Globe Pequot, the trade division of
The Rowman & Littlefield Publishing Group, Inc.
4501 Forbes Blvd., Ste. 200
Lanham, MD 20706
www.stackpolebooks.com

Distributed by NATIONAL BOOK NETWORK
800-462-6420

Originally published in French, *Poupées au Crochet & Leur Garde-robe*, Zess
Copyright © Les Editions de Saxe (France) 2017

Patterns: Zess
Photos: Zess
Technical drawings: Céline Cantat
Page layout: Anne Roule
Translation: Nancy Gingrich, Mithril Translations

British Library Cataloguing in Publication Information available

Library of Congress Cataloging-in-Publication Data available

Names: Zess, Jessica, author.
Title: Crochet cuties : patterns for 24 dolls and 60 clothes and
    accessories / Zess ; translation, Nancy Gingrich, Mithril Translations.
Other titles: Poupées au crochet & leur garde-robe. English
Description: Guilford, Connecticut : Stackpole Books, [2021] | Translation
    of: Poupées au crochet & leur garde-robe. | Summary: "These adorable
    dolls are fun to crochet and adorn in infinite ways! Once you learn to
    make the basic doll, you can change the features, hair, and head
    adornment to make a variety of characters, each with their own
    personality"– Provided by publisher.
Identifiers: LCCN 2020054152 (print) | LCCN 2020054153 (ebook) | ISBN
    9780811739429 (paperback) | ISBN 9780811769396 (epub)
Subjects: LCSH: Doll clothes. | Crocheting–Patterns.
Classification: LCC TT175.7 .Z4713 2021 (print) | LCC TT175.7 (ebook) |
    DDC 746.43/4041–dc23
LC record available at https://lccn.loc.gov/2020054152
LC ebook record available at https://lccn.loc.gov/2020054153

∞™ The paper used in this publication meets the minimum requirements of
American National Standard for Information Sciences–Permanence of Paper
for Printed Library Materials, ANSI/NISO Z39.48-1992.

First Edition

CONTENTS

ABOUT THE AUTHOR

Jessica, alias Zess in her blog, adores vintage decor, loves fashion, and has a ~~slight~~ yarn addiction. She put all of these ingredients into this book, bringing some up-to-date flair to crochet! She shares her world with photos and stories about her daily life as a mom, along with good tips and DIY projects, on her blog at www.zess.fr, which she has had for 14 years now!

Often found with camera in hand, she lives (on love and coffee) in the south of France with her husband and her daughter, Lily-Rose.

Look for her first book published by Stackpole Books, *Crochet for Girls*.

The blog

INTRODUCTION

Cute, sweet, romantic, or funny, these dolls have plenty of surprises in store with all their little outfits.

This book offers a basic doll pattern with a wide variety of items to personalize it and give it character. The doll can have many different looks depending on the eye, nose, and mouth styles selected. And there are many clothing options to choose from, with an infinite number of combinations!

Size of the doll (depending on how you crochet, this may vary somewhat):

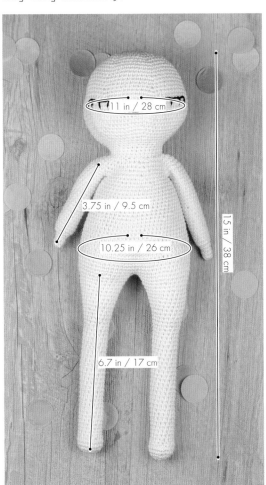

You will first need to decide on the look of the doll.

To do this:

1. Crochet the basic doll, being sure to use a 2.5 mm (US size B-1 or C-2) crochet hook; otherwise the doll will be too large (and will need to go on a diet to fit into the clothes!) or too little (and the clothes will be too big).

2. Decide on the facial features (eyes, nose, and mouth).

3. Choose a hairstyle or a head covering. It is also possible to sew the hair directly onto the head.

4. Crochet an outfit, picking from the many clothing patterns provided.

Note: All clothing is put on from the feet up.

5. Make another doll!

Then share your creations on social media with the hashtag #lespoupeesdezess.

THE DOLLS

VIOLET

We'll start off with sweet Violet, also known as the princess. Thanks to her decisively dainty and romantic wardrobe, she just melts our hearts in this diaphanous tutu and soft sweater. Her round little tummy comes from her love of tasty treats!

She will for sure charm all the little girls!

Specifics: Basic Doll, page 41; Long Princess Hair, page 64; Ruffled Collar Sweater, page 82; No-Sew Tulle Tutu, page 100; Pom-Pom Booties, page 113

JOSETTE

Josette is very creative when it comes to putting together a look that has pizzazz! She is wearing a top dotted with the colors of the rainbow and a straight skirt with knit-like ribbing.

To rein in the curls in her pretty mop of hair, she is sporting her must-have accessory: a very cozy bulky-stitch cap.

Josette is great, but let's not talk to her about Greta; that bugs her—good heavens!

Specifics: Basic Doll, page 41; Curly Hair, page 63; Easy Hat, page 52; Multicolor Bead T-Shirt, page 76; Ribbed Skirt, page 97; Pom-Pom Booties, page 113; Backpack, page 120

PIA

Click, got it! You guessed it—Pia is a photographer. This pretty redhead is understated and refined in her glam lace blouse paired with a button-down A-line skirt. As for her beauty routine, she wears a lot of mascara and never goes out without a touch of lipstick (and her camera, of course!).

Specifics: Basic Doll, page 41; Double Buns, page 62; Fabric Hair Ribbon, page 61; Lace Top, page 79; Striped Skirt, page 99; Ribbed Booties, page 113

SALOMÉ

Welcome to the retro world of Salomé! A total fan of everything vintage, she spends her time bargain hunting at garage sales for old accessories that she brings home in her large bag. Her best find? This granny square jacket, for sure!

And look, she even dares to expose a bit of her bum—how cheeky!

Specifics: Basic Doll, page 41; Large Bun, page 60; Fabric Hair Ribbon, page 61; Retro Granny Jacket, page 67; Torn Jeans, page 90; Fairy Shoes, page 117; Shoulder Bag, page 120

GRETA

Greta is Josette's roommate, but you won't see them together very often for a good reason: they don't get along very well!

A crime fiction author with an unbridled imagination, Greta spends hours in front of the computer screen and takes her big notebook full of ideas with her everywhere, just in case. To add a twist to her fairly classic look, Greta wears a bold top hat. And when she's a little cold (if Josette decides to open the windows at 11:16 p.m. just to annoy her, for example), she switches her mohair blouse for a fuzzy faux fur jacket that suits her perfectly, don't you think?

Specifics: Basic Doll with T-Shirt, page 41; Frizzy Pigtails, page 59; Top Hat, page 58; Fuzzy Faux Fur Jacket, page 69; Empire Sweater, page 88; Torn Jeans, page 90; Ballet Flats, page 117

AGATHA

Sweet and a bit shy, Agatha is the confidante of this group of girlfriends. She gives out wise advice and, cross her heart, never spills secrets. Do you need a "worry doll" next to your pillow? Agatha is here just for you!

It's probably not necessary to point out that her favorite color is dusty rose!

Specifics: Basic Doll, page 41; Bobble Bonnet, page 52; Winter Dress, page 103; Ballet Flats, page 117

DOMI

Domi has a B&B where she likes to spend time tweaking her decor.
She proudly wears an embroidered "LOVE" on her pullover because, well,
for her, love is what it's all about. Oh, and lipstick, too!

Specifics: Basic Doll, page 41; Double Buns, page 62; Hair Bow, page 125; Embroidered Granite Stitch
Pullover, page 86; Zigzag Skirt, page 100; Fringed Booties, page 113

HYACINTH & ROSEMARY

Let's make a detour through the garden to find Hyacinth and Rosemary, the (pretend) twins. Inseparable, they love to wear the same outfits in different colors! Classic and rather sensible, they always wear a perfect bun adorned with a coordinating fabric ribbon. A pretty twosome who prove that each doll can really have her own personality.

Specifics: Basic Doll, page 41; Large Bun, page 60; Fabric Hair Ribbon, page 61; Granite Stitch Pullover with Peter Pan Collar, page 86; Scalloped-Hem Skirt, page 98; Ballet Flats, page 117

FAWNTINE

We have all fallen for Fawntine's sweet little face, which is never seen anywhere unless surrounded by her lucky hat and her nice, warm bobble pullover.

Just remember, never make her watch *Bambi* . . .

Specifics: Basic Doll, page 41; Deer Beanie, page 55; Bobble Pullover, page 83; Fabric Skirt, page 102; Fringed Booties, page 113

DINA

Curious and very talkative, Dina is never at a loss for words! But no one holds it against her; she is so cute with her bunny slippers and her little overalls! This incorrigible chatterbox always tries to discover what secrets Agatha is keeping.

Specifics: Basic Doll with Yellow T-Shirt, page 41; Double Buns, page 62; Hair Bow, page 125; Shortalls with Pockets, page 110; Bunny Slippers, page 115

JO & ANNA

The essential wardrobe item for this pair? A nice, cozy marled jacket!
Whether with the large, flower-adorned collar for Jo, paired with bobble
shorts, or with the hood for Anna, paired with a fabric skirt, this jacket
makes them irresistible, along with their darling round eyes. Their favorite
pastime? Gardening, of course!

Specifics for Jo:
Basic Doll with Striped Tights, page 41; Bear Cub Beanie, page 55; "Brrr" Jacket with Large Collar, page 72; Bobble Shorts, page 89; Ballet Flats, page 117

Specifics for Anna:
Basic Doll, page 41; Square Cut Hair, page 62; Hooded "Brrr" Jacket, page 72; Fabric Skirt, page 102; Laced Booties, page 113

NINA

With her square cut and flawless bangs, Nina polishes her look down to the last detail. Like a good fashionista, she spends a lot of time in front of the mirror. Today, she opted for the ruffled collar sweater with a graphic print skirt. As for accessories, her black and white marled bag goes with her everywhere.

Her friends have some serious fashion envy; plus Nina never wants to lend anything! Her (very) peculiar trait: she never says either yes or no. So, you may have difficulty getting to know her (we never said she was clever . . .).

Specifics: Basic Doll, page 41; Square Cut Hair, page 62; Hair Bow, page 125; Ruffled Collar Sweater, page 82; Fabric Skirt, page 102; Striped Socks, page 115; Fringed Bag, page 121

LOLY

Loly is the girl who has written "lol" more than anyone else. A prankster and constantly in a good mood, she always has a joke up her sleeve. Her motto: love, joy, and confetti! Her hair is often a mess (pink now, but that changes all the time). Her dress code: mixing colors that sparkle!

For you, she even got out her party hat—how about that?

Specifics: Basic Doll with Turquoise T-Shirt, page 41; Long Hair, page 60; Party Hat, page 58; Bib Overalls, page 96; Fairy Shoes, page 117

With his mischievous grin and sweet freckles (according to my daughter, Lily-Rose, he would rather be allergic to carrots), Abbott is the most adorable little rabbit!

He is wearing a mustard yellow cardigan with a scalloped collar paired with textured joggers that show off his striped tights. The final touch? His rabbit cap, obviously!

Don't leave him too close to any screens—Abbott is hooked on television shows and will binge watch whole seasons without stopping!

Specifics: Basic Doll with Striped Tights, page 41; Bunny Beanie, page 55; Cable Twist Cardigan, page 70; Textured Joggers, page 93; Shoes with Bow, page 116

PIKI

The romantic charm of this diaphanous mohair dress is accentuated by colorful notes from the scalloped collar and cuffed booties.

The delightful Piki loves mojitos, braids, and cacti.

Specifics: Basic doll, page 41; Braids, page 62; Hair Bows, page 125; "Soft and Sweet" Dress, page 104; Scalloped Collar, page 119; Cuffed Booties, page 113

MARY-SUN

Beach, shells, and bikini for Mary-Sun! It seems that the ocean air curls
her hair, styled here with a fabric headband. Her cute swimsuit is
trimmed with little ruffles.

Do you smell the fragrance of sunscreen lingering around her?

Specifics: Basic Doll, page 41; Curly Hair, page 63; Bikini, page 111; Satchel, page 121

MARGUERITE

We love her, a little, a lot, passionately, forever and ever!

A math teacher, Marguerite gives herself a well-deserved break each weekend and goes to pick flowers, far away from equations. She often ends up falling asleep on her pretty throw blanket (composed of isosceles triangles, she made sure, obviously!).

Despite all the time in the sun, she still manages to keep her porcelain complexion!

Specifics: Basic Doll, page 41; Dotted Bonnet, page 54; Romper, page 108; Shoes with Bow, page 116, Triangle Throw Blanket, page 125

TINA

With her colorful outfit, Tina has a very rosy outlook!

She is, however, sensitive to the cold and always has a cozy jacket nearby.
It's impossible to resist her sweet chevron and checkered dress and the
cute crown of flowers in her hair!

Specifics: Basic Doll, page 41; Large Bun, page 60; Flower Crown, page 122; Candy Pink Dress, page 106;
Furry Shepherd's Cardigan, page 65; Laced Booties, page 113

AVERY & EMORY

Girls or boys? It's up to you to decide!
Sensitive to the cold, Avery layers a cozy vest over a classic sailor sweater.
Emory reveals a bit of skin wearing this bold crop top!

Specifics for Avery:
Basic Doll, page 41; Pointy Pixie Bonnet, page 53; Sailor Sweater, page 85; Furry Shepherd's Vest, page 65;
Shorts (from Overalls), page 96; Booties (Basic Pattern), page 113

Specifics for Emory:
Basic Doll with Striped Tights, page 41; Crop Top, page 80; Ribbed Bloomers, page 94; Ribbed Booties,
page 113

SOPHIA

Lounging on some soft cushions while listening to very (very) loud music is Sophia's favorite way to relax. She is the queen of procrastination! As for her style, Sophia is keen on comfy clothes, like these fun, cozy shorts paired with a poncho that wraps around her like a blanket, along with some bunny slippers to keep her little toes nice and warm!

Specifics: Basic Doll, page 41; Short Pigtails, page 60; Cape, page 75; Fuzzy Shorts, page 92; Bunny Slippers, page 115

ROSIE

Oh, pretty Rosie! We just love her whole cotton-candy look,
to be consumed in moderation!

With her openwork top and ruffled skirt in shades of pink,
Rosie shows us that "pink is the new black"!

Specifics: Basic Doll, page 41; Frizzy Pigtails, page 59; Top Hat, page 58; Tulle Ruff, page 119; Tricolor Top,
page 77; Ruffled Skirt, page 102; Shoes with Bow, page 116

–
CROCHET
BASICS
–

STITCHES

CROCHET

Slipknot

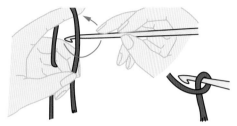

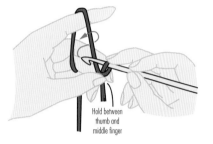

Hold between thumb and middle finger

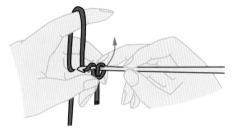

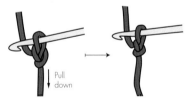

Pull down

Step 1: Put the hook behind the yarn and turn the hook as indicated by the arrow.

Step 2: Hold the loop just made between your thumb and middle finger. Then bring the yarn over the hook as shown in the drawing.

Step 3: Draw the yarn caught in the hook through the loop.

Step 4: Pull the end of the yarn down to tighten the loop just made.

Magic Circle

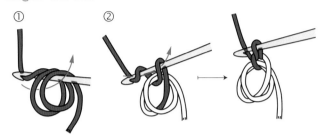

Step 1: Wrap the yarn around your index finger twice, insert the hook through the circle, and draw the yarn through.

Step 2: Bring the yarn over the hook and draw the yarn through the loop on the hook, completing the circle.

Note: At the end of the next round, pull on the yarn tail to tighten the magic circle.

Chain Stitch

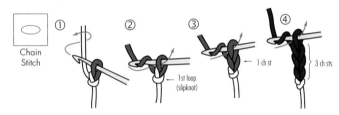

Chain Stitch

1st loop (slipknot)

1 ch st

3 ch sts

Step 1: Bring yarn over the hook as indicated by the arrow.

Step 2: Draw the yarn through the loop that is already on your hook to make the first chain stitch.

Step 3: Yarn over and draw through the first chain to make the second chain stitch.

Step 4: Repeat step 3 as many times as indicated.

Slip Stitch

Slip Stitch

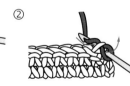

Step 1: At the beginning of the row, insert hook in the first stitch as indicated by the arrow.

Step 2: Bring yarn over hook and pull it through the stitch, following the arrow. One slip stitch completed.

Step 3: Insert hook in the second stitch as indicated by the arrow.

Step 4: The slip stitch has a tendency to be crocheted rather tightly, so I recommend lengthening the loop slightly to keep the stitch a bit more loose and stretchy.

Single Crochet

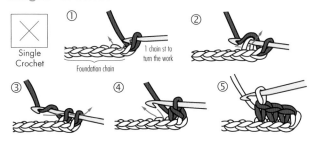

Step 1: Begin with one chain stitch to turn the work, and then insert the hook where indicated in the drawing.

Step 2: Yarn over and pull it through the stitch as indicated by the arrow.

Step 3: Yarn over and pull it through both loops on the hook. That completes one single crochet.

Step 4: Repeat steps 1 to 3 for each single crochet indicated, omitting the turning chain stitch and inserting hook into next stitch to begin.

Step 5: Here, three single crochets are completed.

Half Double Crochet

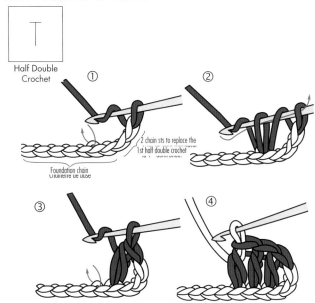

Step 1: Begin with two chain stitches to replace the first half double crochet. Bring yarn over the hook and insert it into the fourth chain from the hook.

Step 2: Yarn over the hook and pull it through the stitch, yarn over the hook again and pull it through all the loops on the hook. That completes one half double crochet.

Step 3: Repeat steps 1 and 2 for each half double crochet indicated, omitting the turning chains and inserting the hook into the next stitch.

Step 4: Here, four half double crochets are completed, counting the two chain stitches as the first half double crochet.

Double Crochet

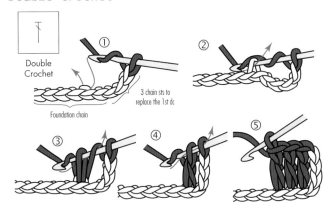

Step 1: Begin with three chain stitches to replace the first double crochet. Then bring yarn over the hook and insert it where indicated by the arrow in the drawing.

Step 2: Bring yarn over the hook and pull it through the stitch, following the arrow.

Step 3: Yarn over the hook again and pull it through the first two loops on the hook.

Step 4: Yarn over once more and pull it through two remaining loops on the hook. That completes one double crochet.

Step 5: Repeat steps 1 to 4 for each double crochet indicated, omitting the three turning chains and inserting the hook into the next stitch. Shown here, four double crochets are completed, including the three chain stitches as the first double crochet.

CROCHET BASICS

Triple Crochet

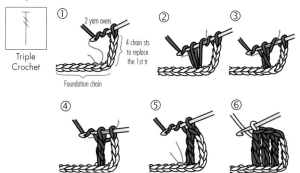

Increases

The general principle is to make two identical stitches into the same stitch. Below is an example of a single crochet increase; for a double crochet increase, you would work two double crochets into the same space, and do the same for other stitches.

Example of a single crochet increase

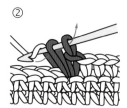
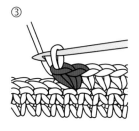

Step 1: Begin with four chain stitches to replace the first triple crochet, and then yarn over twice and insert the hook where indicated by the arrow.

Step 2: Yarn over and pull it through the stitch. Yarn over again and pull it through two loops.

Step 3: Yarn over again and pull it through two loops on the hook.

Step 4: Yarn over once more and pull it through the two remaining loops on the hook. That completes one triple crochet.

Step 5: Repeat steps 1 to 4 for each triple crochet indicated, omitting the four chain stitches and inserting hook into the next stitch.

Step 6: Here, four triple crochets are completed, counting the four chain stitches as the first triple crochet.

Step 1: Insert the hook into the same stitch in which you just made a single crochet.

Step 2: Yarn over and pull it through the stitch, yarn over again and pull it through the two loops on the hook.

Step 3: This completes one single crochet increase.

Back Loop Only Stitches

A ridge is created on the right side when working into the BACK LOOP ONLY of a stitch.

Example of single crochet into the back loop

Decreases

Single crochet 2 together

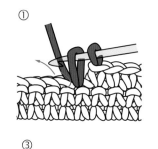

Step 1: Chain 1, and then make a single crochet inserting the hook into the BACK LOOP ONLY (shown in color on the drawing) of the stitch from the previous round (or row).

Repeat this step for subsequent stitches.

Step 1: Insert the hook into a stitch, yarn over and pull up a loop through the stitch, and then repeat this step in the next stitch (= two incomplete single crochets).

Step 2: Yarn over and pull it through all the loops on the hook.

Step 3: This completes a single crochet decrease (there is one less single crochet).

Invisible single crochet decrease

Step 1: Insert the hook into the front loop of the first stitch.

Step 2: Insert the hook into the back loop of the next stitch.

Step 3: Yarn over and pull it through the two stitches on the hook.

Step 4: Yarn over and pull it through the two remaining loops on the hook.

To put it simply, this is like making a standard single crochet in the front and back loop of two consecutive stitches.

Note: It is also possible to make a decrease following this same principle but replacing the single crochets with double crochets. Simply do a yarn over before inserting the hook into the front and the back loops of two consecutive stitches, and then complete the double crochet as usual.

Double crochet 2 together

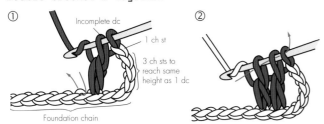

Step 1: Crochet an incomplete double crochet (leave the last loop on the hook), yarn over, and then insert hook into the next chain as indicated by the arrow.

Step 2: Crochet another incomplete double crochet, and then yarn over and draw through all loops remaining on the hook at once. One double crochet 2 together completed.

Back Post Double Crochet

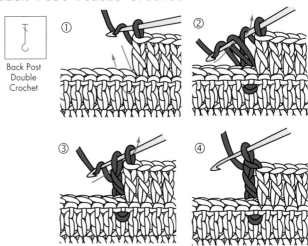

Back Post Double Crochet

Step 1: Yarn over, and then insert the hook from the back completely around the post of the stitch from the previous row (or round), as indicated by the arrow.

Step 2: Bring yarn over the hook and draw it around the post to the back, and then yarn over again and pull it through the first two loops on the hook as indicated by the arrow.

Step 3: Yarn over and bring it through the two remaining loops on the hook, drawing it out a little longer than normal.

Step 4: That completes one back post double crochet. The top "V" of the double crochet from the previous row (or round) is seen on the right side and the newly made double crochet appears raised on the BACK side of the work.

CROCHET BASICS

Front Post Double Crochet

① 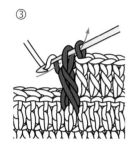　②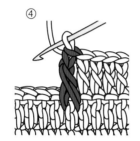

③ 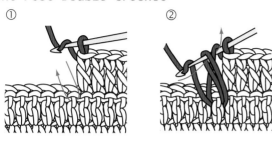　④

Step 1: Yarn over, and then insert the hook from the front completely around the post of the stitch from the previous row (or round) as indicated by the arrow.

Step 2: Bring yarn over the hook and draw it around the post to the front, and then yarn over again and pull it through the first two loops on the hook as indicated by the arrow.

Step 3: Yarn over and bring it through the two remaining loops to complete the double crochet.

Step 4: That completes one front post double crochet. The top "V" of the double crochet from the previous row (or round) is seen on the wrong side. The newly made double crochet appears raised on the FRONT side of the work.

Single Crochet Bobble

Repeat five times into the same stitch *insert hook into the stitch, yarn over and pull through the stitch, yarn over and pull through one loop on the hook*, and then yarn over and draw it through all six loops on the hook.

The bobble forms on the reverse side of the work after the next single crochet is made.

Abbreviations

BLO	back loop only
ch	chain
ch st	chain stitch
dc	double crochet
dc2tog	double crochet 2 together
dec	decrease
FLO	front loop only
hdc	half double crochet
inc	increase

EMBROIDERY STITCHES

Running Stitch

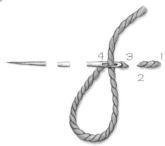

Chain Stitch

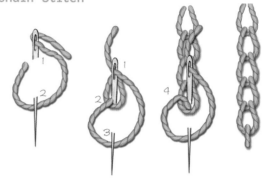

Stem Stitch

Straight Stitch

pm	place marker
rnd	round
sc	single crochet
sc2tog	single crochet 2 together
sl st	slip stitch
st(s)	stitch(es)
tr	triple crochet
x	times
yo	yarn over

TECHNIQUES

Working in a Spiral

This technique creates a circle with incomplete rounds, like the continuous spiral of a screw. At the end of the round, crochet directly into the first stitch of the previous round without closing it with a slip stitch.

Note: Place a stitch marker (ring or contrasting yarn) in the first stitch of the round and continue to move it to the first stitch of each new round (not always indicated in the directions).

Working around a Foundation Chain

Begin by working the number of chain stitches required, and then crochet into the top loop of each chain stitch from right to left, turn to the other side of the chain, and crochet into the lower loop of the chain stitches, returning to the first stitch. Then close with a slip stitch into the first stitch (only when working in the round).

Example

Working around a foundation chain

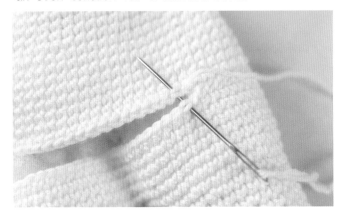

2. Work the stitches from right to left (here in sc) in the top loop of the chain stitches.

1. First stitch at x sts from the hook (here 1 sc in the 2nd chain from the hook).

3. Move to the other side of the chain.

Foundation chain (here 7 ch sts).

4. Work the sts from left to right (here in sc) in the lower loop of the chain stitches.

5. Close with 1 sl st in the first st (= working in the round), or not (= working in a spiral). Then continue according to directions.

Key

∘ **Chain 1:** Yo, pull through loop on the hook.

× **1 single crochet:** Insert hook in st, yo and pull through the st, yo and pull through all loops on the hook.

Changing Colors at End of Row or Round

Crochet normally in the starting color, and then, at the last stitch of the row (or round), change the color by working the last step of the stitch in the new color.

Joining with Whipstitch

Position the two pieces to be joined opposite each other and insert a yarn needle threaded with the yarn under one or both loops of a stitch from the first piece and then through the corresponding stitch of the second piece. Repeat this step as many times as necessary, being sure to maintain an even tension for a uniform seam.

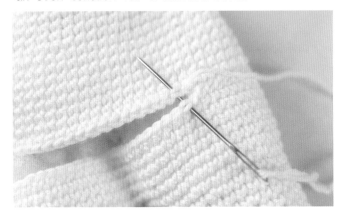

Finishing Your Work

In this book, each time it says "cut yarn," work 1 chain stitch and then cut the yarn long enough to be able to weave it in or to use it later for sewing.

Embellishments

Tassels

Step 1: Wrap yarn around a thick piece of cardboard until it seems enough for the tassel, and then slide a piece of yarn underneath the top end and tie it off. Use scissors to cut the bottom of the strands.

Step 2: Wrap another piece of yarn several times around the tassel near the top end and tie off tightly.

CROCHET BASICS

Pom-poms

Cut two identical templates from stiff cardboard (make a disk with the desired outside diameter and cut out a small circle in the center).

Step 1: Place the two cardboard templates together. Then, using a needle, wrap the yarn around the two templates as shown in figure 1.

Step 2: Slide the tip of the scissors between the two templates and under the yarn, and cut the strands all the way around the edge of the disk.

Step 3: Slide a piece of yarn between the two cardboard templates. Tie it tightly and double knot it. Remove the templates, and then use scissors to even out the shape of the pom-pom.

Fringe

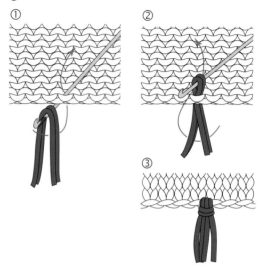

Step 1: Prepare the number of strands needed for the fringe. Then, on the wrong side of the work, insert the hook into the stitch where you want to place fringe and pull the strands through this stitch to form a small loop.

Step 2: With the hook, bring the strands through the loop (see arrow).

Step 3: The fringe is now finished on the right side of the work.

BASIC DOLL

> **The doll is worked in 3 parts:**
>
> **1.** the head (worked top down)
> **2.** the chest (worked top down), followed by the arms
> **3.** the legs (worked bottom up)
> Then all the parts are sewn together.
>
> *Note: Colored marker = piece of*
> *yarn or locking safety pin-type marker*

SUPPLIES

· Bergère de France Coton Fifty yarn (#2 fine weight; 4 ply; 50% cotton, 50% acrylic; 153 yd/140 m per 1.8 oz/50 g) in the following colors: Coco (white), Berlingot (pink), Zan (black), and your preferred colors for the versions with T-shirt (or long-sleeved top) or striped tights.
Note: For the version without T-shirt, you will need 2 balls of white.
· Needle and black sewing thread (optional, for thin eyelashes)
· Flexible wire (optional, for firmer, posable arms)
· Stuffing
· 2.5 mm (US B-1 or C-2) crochet hook
· Yarn needle
· Stitch markers

STITCHES AND TECHNIQUES

· Magic circle, chain stitch, single crochet, invisible decrease, single crochet increase: **see Stitches, page 34.**
· Working around a foundation chain, working in a spiral, joining with whipstitch: **see Techniques, page 39.**
· Stem stitch, straight stitch: **see Embroidery Stitches, page 38.**

INSTRUCTIONS

The number between parentheses is the number of stitches at the end of the rnd (or row).

Head

Note: The head is not completely round. Therefore, we start with a foundation chain and work around it.

With white, ch 7 and work in a spiral.

Rnd 1: 1 sc in the 2nd ch from hook (pm), 5 sc, move to the other side of the chain, 6 sc. (12 sts)

Rnd 2: Repeat 6 times *1 sc, 1 inc*. (18 sts)

Rnd 3: Repeat 6 times *2 sc, 1 inc*. (24 sts)

Rnd 4: Repeat 6 times *3 sc, 1 inc*. (30 sts)

Rnd 5: Repeat 6 times *4 sc, 1 inc*. (36 sts)

Rnd 6: Repeat 6 times *5 sc, 1 inc*. (42 sts)

Rnd 7: Repeat 6 times *6 sc, 1 inc*. (48 sts)

Rnd 8: Repeat 6 times *7 sc, 1 inc*. (54 sts)

Rnd 9: Repeat 6 times *8 sc, 1 inc*. (60 sts)

Rnds 10-12: 60 sc. (60 sts)

Rnd 13: Repeat 6 times *9 sc, 1 inc*. (66 sts)

Rnds 14-15: 66 sc. (66 sts)

Rnd 16: Repeat 6 times *10 sc, 1 inc*. (72 sts)

Rnd 17: Repeat 6 times *11 sc, 1 inc*. (78 sts)

Rnd 18: Repeat 6 times *12 sc, 1 inc*. (84 sts)

✓ **For embroidered eyes:** Place colored marker on 15th st and 29th st.

✓ **For round eyes:** Place colored marker on 14th st and 30th st.

Rnds 19-23: 84 sc. (84 sts)

Rnd 24: Repeat 6 times *12 sc, 1 invisible dec*. (78 sts)

Rnd 25: Repeat 6 times *11 sc, 1 invisible dec*. (72 sts)

Rnd 26: Repeat 6 times *10 sc, 1 invisible dec*. (66 sts)

Rnd 27: Repeat 6 times *9 sc, 1 invisible dec*. (60 sts)

DO NOT CUT YARN.

✓ Remove hook, place colored **marker** in the loop to keep work from unraveling, and leave working yarn to be picked up later.

Making the Face

This step is very important, as this is when the doll's personality will come out. Don't hesitate to combine elements as you wish!

Eyes

Remember that the head is not round, and therefore it is important to properly position it facing you, horizontally.

The eyes are placed between Rnds 18 and 19 (colored markers), spaced 14 sts apart for embroidered eyes and 16 sts apart for the round safety eyes. The markers indicate placement of inner corner of the eye (see photo).

Embroidered Eyes

In black with the yarn needle, make a couple knots at the end of the yarn, and then embroider in stem stitch on the same line, in the little holes between the two rounds.

Horizontal line, used as base for all embroidered eyelashes

Insert the needle from the wrong side and bring up at the marker. Repeat 3 times *skip 1 st, insert (A) and bring up the needle at skipped st (B)*, and then insert in next st without skipping a st. DO NOT CUT THE THREAD (see photo).

For two large outside lashes

Bring up the needle 2 rounds above and slightly at a slant. Insert needle on horizontal line, and then bring up the needle 2 rounds above for the second lash and repeat.

Additional smaller lashes: Make the 2 large lashes described above, and then repeat three times; *bring up the needle a bit farther down along the horizontal line, and then insert in a st in the round above*.

Lashes facing down: Bring up the needle 2 rounds below and slightly at a slant. Insert needle at horizontal line; repeat with 3 straight lashes, and then finish with a last lash a bit slanted.

Turn head to wrong side and knot yarn twice to secure.

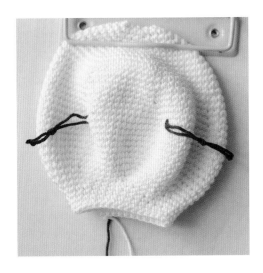

Embroidered eyes version

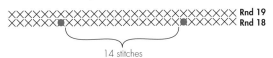

14 stitches

Rnd 19
Rnd 18

Key

● 1 marker.

× **1 single crochet:** Insert hook in st, yo and pull through the st, yo and pull through all loops on the hook.

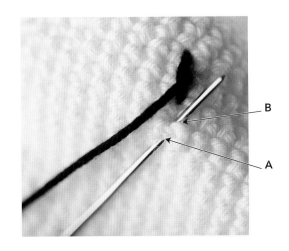

43

Safety eyes version

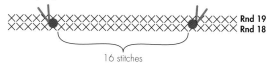

Rnd 19
Rnd 18

16 stitches

Key

— 1 straight stitch

• 1 safety eye

✕ 1 single crochet: Insert hook in st, yo and pull through the st, yo and pull through all loops on the hook.

Animal nose version

(b)◀ — Top of nose

(a) — Bottom of nose

Key

◀ Cut yarn.

○ Chain 1: Yo, pull through loop on the hook.

⤸ 1 single crochet increase: Work 2 sc into the same st.

Animal mouth version

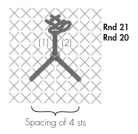

Rnd 21
Rnd 20

(1) (2)

Spacing of 4 sts

Key

— 1 straight stitch

● Marker

Safety Eyes Version

With the sewing needle and some doubled black sewing thread, first make 2 straight sts for the eyelashes where marker is placed. Use a plastic eye (without fastening it) to see where to best place the lashes. Secure thread with a few knots on wrong side. Now insert and clip on safety eyes at markers.

Notes:
- *For thicker lashes, use Coton Fifty yarn.*
- *To be safe for babies, don't use plastic eyes; rather, embroider round eyes in Coton Fifty.*

Nose and Mouth

Animal Nose

Note: Leave a length of thread at the beginning (a) and end (b) of work for sewing.

In pink, with 2.5 mm (US B-1 or C-2) crochet hook, chain 2, and then work 2 sc in the 2nd ch. Do not make ch st to end; cut yarn, leaving a long tail.

ASSEMBLY

Identify the 2 sts at the center of the 14 or 16 sts between the eyes. Use 2 ball head pins to mark the holes located on the outsides of these 2 stitches, between Rnds 20 and 21.

Step 1 (adding the nose): Thread yarn (b) into yarn needle, insert it at pin no. 1, and then bring needle up 2 sts farther at pin no. 2. Bring needle through the ch st at bottom of the nose and reinsert needle in the same st. Make 2 knots on the wrong side and cut the yarn.

Step 2 (mouth): Thread yarn (a) for the nose into yarn needle, insert into stitch 2 rounds below vertically (blue marker on the drawing), bring up needle 2 rounds below and 2 sts to the left, reinsert in st no. 1, bring needle back up 2 rounds below and 2 sts to the right, and reinsert into st no. 1. Make 2 knots on the wrong side and cut the yarn.

Smiling Mouth

Find the 2 center stitches between the 14 or 16 sts separating the eyes, and use 2 ball head pins to mark the holes on either side of these 2 sts between Rnds 21 and 22.

With pink, make a knot at the end of the yarn. Bring needle up at a marker (in circles on the illustration), and then with yarn on the right side, insert it at the second marker. Bring needle up 1 round above and slightly at a diagonal, and then reinsert at the second marker. Bring needle up at the first marker and insert 1 round above and slightly at a diagonal.

Knot twice on wrong side and cut the yarn.

Small Mouth

Mark the 2 center stitches between the 14 or 16 sts separating the eyes, and use 2 ball head pins to mark the holes located on either side of these 2 sts between Rnds 21 and 22.

With pink, make a knot at the end of the yarn. Repeat 4 times *bring needle up at first marker (in circle on the illustration), insert at the second marker, bringing yarn over the top side*. Then, for the corners of the lips, make 1 horizontal straight st on each side, 1 st in length.

Cheeks

To make freckles, thread needle with Coton Fifty (in Nectarine, for example) and make a knot at the end of the yarn. Working from the wrong side, bring needle up in the cheek area, and then bring back to wrong side, making a tiny stitch. Insert yarn again from the wrong side a bit farther away and repeat.

Finishing the Head

Once all the embroidery is completed, put hook back in the stitch with colored marker at Rnd 27, and continuing with the white yarn, finish the head as follows:

Rnd 28: Repeat 6 times *8 sc, sc2tog*. (54 sts)

Rnd 29: 3 sc, sc2tog, 5 sc, repeat 4 times *sc2tog, 6 sc*, sc2tog, 5 sc, sc2tog, 3 sc. (47 sts)

Rnd 30: 3 sc, sc2tog, 4 sc, repeat 2 times *sc2tog, 5 sc*, sc2tog, 4 sc, repeat 2 times *sc2tog, 5 sc*, sc2tog, 2 sc. (40 sts)

Rnd 31: 2 sc, repeat 7 times *sc2tog, 3 sc*, sc2tog, 1 sc. (32 sts)

Rnds 32–34: 32 sc. (32 sts)

At the end of Rnd 34, cut yarn, leaving a long tail for sewing.

Stuff the head tightly.

Smiling mouth

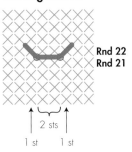

Rnd 22
Rnd 21

2 sts
1 st   1 st

Key

— 1 straight stitch

● 1 marker (= pin)

Small mouth

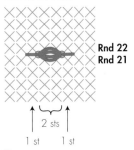

Rnd 22
Rnd 21

2 sts
1 st   1 st

Key

— 1 straight stitch

● 1 marker (= pin)

Main Body

With white, chain 32 and work in a spiral.
✓ Place colored marker (to use for joining) on the 29th st.

Rnd 1: Repeat 8 times *1 inc, 3 sc*. (40 sts)

> *Note: To make a T-shirt, change colors at the end of Rnd 1 in the last st. Make 2 tight knots on the wrong side with the 2 colors.*

Rnd 2: 3 sc, 1 inc, repeat 7 times *4 sc, 1 inc*, 1 sc. (48 sts)

Rnd 3: Repeat 8 times *1 inc, 5 sc*. (56 sts)

Rnd 4: 4 sc, 1 inc, repeat 7 times *6 sc, 1 inc*, 2 sc. (64 sts)

Rnd 5: Repeat 8 times *1 inc, 7 sc*. (72 sts)

Dividing for Arms

Rnd 6: 2 sc, skip 14 sts (arm), 22 sc, skip 14 sts (arm), 20 sc. (44 sts)

Rnd 7: 1 sc, 2 inc, repeat 2 times *6 sc, 1 inc*, 6 sc, 2 inc, repeat 2 times *6 sc, 1 inc*, 5 sc. (52 sts)

Rnds 8–15: 52 sc. (52 sts)

Rnd 16: Repeat 2 times *1 inc, 8 sc, 1 inc, 7 sc, 1 inc, 8 sc*. (58 sts)

Rnd 17: Repeat 2 times *8 sc, 1 inc*, repeat 2 times *9 sc, 1 inc*, 8 sc, 1 inc, 9 sc, 1 inc, 1 sc. (64 sts)

Rnds 18–23: 64 sc. (64 sts)

Rnd 24: Repeat 4 times *15 sc, 1 inc*. (68 sts)
✓ Place colored marker (to use for joining) on the 60th st of Rnd 24. Cut yarn.

Arms

> *Note: Continue to work in spiral.*

With white (or with T-shirt color), attach yarn to the 1st skipped stitch from Rnd 6, leaving a tail to sew the underarm.

Rnd 1: Ch 1, 1 sc (pm), 13 sc. (14 sts)

Make 2 small sts at the underarm with the needle and yarn tail left above.

Rnds 2–5: 14 sc. (14 sts)

✓ **For the T-shirt version:** Pick up white yarn again at the end of Rnd 5.

Rnds 6–22: 14 sc. (14 sts)

✓ **For the long-sleeved shirt version:** Continue with the T-shirt color as follows:

Rnds 6–20: 14 sc. (14 sts) Pick up white yarn again at the end of Rnd 20.

Rnds 21–22 (white): 14 sc. (14 sts)

Hands

Rnd 23: 7 sc2tog. (7 sts)

Rnds 24-26: 7 sc. (7 sts) *(Tip: Crochet 21 sts in a row so as to not have to move the marker each round.)*

Cut yarn, leaving a tail.

Closing: Thread the tail of yarn into a tapestry needle and bring it through the 7 sts. Pull to tighten, fasten off, and then hide yarn tail in the arm.

Make a second identical arm, BUT THIS TIME leaving it open.

Legs

Begin with a magic circle, and work in a spiral.

Rnd 1: Ch 1, 1 sc (pm = 1st st), 6 sc. (7 sts)

Rnd 2: 7 inc. (14 sts)

Rnd 3: Repeat 7 times *1 sc, 1 inc*. (21 sts)

Rnds 4-5: 21 sc. (21 sts)

Rnd 6: Repeat 3 times *sc2tog, 2 sc, sc2tog, 1 sc*. (15 sts)

Rnds 7-33 (3.5 in/9 cm): 15 sc. (15 sts)

Rnd 34: 3 sc, 1 inc, 7 sc, 1 inc, 3 sc. (17 sts)

Rnd 35: 1 inc, 7 sc, 1 inc, 8 sc. (19 sts)

Rnds 36-37: 19 sc. (19 sts)

Rnd 38: 4 sc, 1 inc, 9 sc, 1 inc, 4 sc. (21 sts)

Rnds 39-40: 21 sc. (21 sts)

Rnd 41: 1 sc, 1 inc, repeat 2 times *6 sc, 1 inc*, 5 sc. (24 sts)

Rnds 42-43: 24 sc. (24 sts)

Rnd 44: Repeat 3 times *7 sc, 1 inc*. (27 sts)

Rnd 45: 27 sc. (27 sts)

Rnd 46: 1 sc, 1 inc, repeat 2 times *8 sc, 1 inc*, 7 sc. (30 sts)

Rnd 47: Repeat 5 times *5 sc, 1 inc*. (35 sts)

Leave marker in the next st. Cut yarn, leaving a long tail.

Make a second identical leg, BUT DO NOT CUT THE YARN at the end of Rnd 47 and continue as follows to join legs:

Rnd 48: 35 sc on the leg currently being worked, and then continue by also working 35 sts on the 1st leg (begin at marker and remove it). (70 sts)

Rnd 49: 18 sc, sc2tog, 31 sc, sc2tog, 17 sc. (68 sts)

Rnds 50-53: 68 sc. (68 sts)

Cut yarn, leaving a long tail for sewing.

TIP

To make **striped tights**, alternate 2 colors every 3 rounds until Rnd 53.

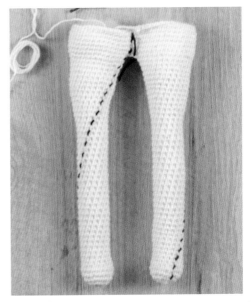

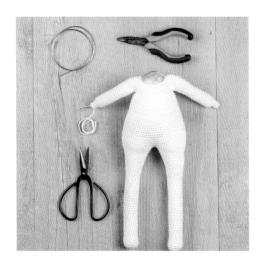

Stuff the legs by sliding in small balls of the stuffing material and pushing to the end with a large crochet hook. Only put in small amounts of stuffing at a time so the legs do not become lumpy, but stuff until firm so the doll can stand up on a shelf, for example.

Assembly with Whipstitch

Make 2 small stitches in between the legs using the yarn from the first leg.

With the longer tail from the legs, sew them to the body as follows:

Insert the needle at the colored marker and then in the last st (from the tail). Continue joining in whipstitch for the remaining 67 stitches.

When you are about 2 in/5 cm from the end of the opening, firmly stuff the area where the legs meet the main body.

Fasten off with a knot; insert needle far into the main body to hide the yarn tail.

Stuff the bottom of the main body BUT NOT THE ARMS.

If adding wire to the arms, bend the tip of the wire so it is nice and rounded. Slide it through the end of the open arm and push it to the far end of the other arm. Cut the wire at the end of the hand, bend that tip as well, and finish sliding it into the arm.

Now close the end of the second arm as for the 1st one using the remaining yarn.

Stuff the top of the body. If you inserted wire, do not stuff the arms; otherwise, stuff the arms at this time.

With the long yarn tail from the head, sew the head to the body:

Insert the needle at the colored marker at the top of the body and then in the last st (from the long tail). Continue joining in whipstitch for the remaining 31 stitches. Before closing, stuff the neck and top of the body firmly.

Fasten off with a knot. Insert the needle far into the head to hide the yarn tail.

Don't hesitate to stuff the body parts tightly. The doll will look prettier and will keep its shape better.

Press a bit on the head to shape it, giving it a lovely, rounded appearance.

CLOTHING &
ACCESSORIES

–
HATS
–

BOBBLE BONNET

INSTRUCTIONS

The number between parentheses is the number of sts at the end of the row. Begin by chaining 54 sts (pm in last ch st).

Row 1: 1 dc in the 5th ch from hook (place colored marker around this dc for sewing on button), 49 dc. (51 sts)
Row 2: Ch 1, repeat 12 times *3 sc, 1 bobble*, 3 sc. (51 sts)
Row 3: 51 dc. (51 sts)
Row 4: Ch 1, 1 sc, repeat 12 times *1 bobble, 3 sc*, 1 bobble, 1 sc. (51 sts)
Row 5: Repeat Row 3.
Row 6: Repeat Row 2.
Row 7: Repeat Row 3.
Row 8: Repeat Row 4.
Row 9: Repeat Row 3.
Row 10: Repeat Row 2. DO NOT CUT YARN.

JOINING AT CENTER BACK

By Sewing
Rnd 11: 25 dc, DO NOT WORK THE REMAINING STS. Cut yarn, leaving a long tail; fold rectangle in half and sew the 25 dc just worked to the 25 unworked sts on the same side.

Without Sewing
Crochet the next row, joining to other side as you go as follows:
Rnd 11: 1 dc, remove hook from loop, insert hook in the last st of the row from right side to wrong side, pull the loop through the st, repeat 24 times *1 dc, remove hook from loop, insert the hook in the next st from front to back, pull the loop through the st*.

Sew the button on at the colored marker. Insert button through the 2 corresponding dc on the other side to button.

EASY HAT

INSTRUCTIONS

The number between parentheses is the number of sts at the end of the rnd.
In pink, start with a magic circle.
Rnd 1: 12 dc, 1 sl st at the marker. (12 sts)
Rnd 2: Repeat 6 times *1 dc, 1 inc*, 1 sl st at the marker. (18 sts)
Rnd 3: Repeat 6 times *2 dc, 1 inc*, 1 sl st at the marker. (24 sts)

Rnd 4: Repeat 6 times *1 inc, 3 dc*, 1 sl st at the marker. (30 sts)

Rnd 5: 2 dc, repeat 5 times *1 inc, 4 dc*, 1 inc, 2 dc, 1 sl st at the marker. (36 sts)

Rnd 6: 1 inc, 35 dc, 1 sl st at the marker, changing to gray yarn. (37 sts)

Rnd 7 (edging): 1 ch st (turning ch), 37 sc.
Cut yarn.

Prepare a pom-pom and attach it at Rnd 2 around the 2 dc of an inc.
Put the cap on the doll's head, a bit toward the back, but so the pom-pom is toward the front.

POINTY PIXIE BONNET

INSTRUCTIONS

The number between parentheses is the number of sts at the end of the row.

Body

With Idéal yarn, and using a 3.5 mm (US E-4) hook, chain 52 sts (leaving a long tail at the beginning for the **tie**).

Row 1: 1 hdc in the 4th ch from hook, 48 hdc. (50 sts)

Rows 2-12: Ch 1 to turn, 50 hdc into the back loop only. (50 sts)

DO NOT CUT THE YARN, ch 1, remove hook and slide a marker into the loop.

With Abakan (or Teddy), and using a 6 mm (US J-10) hook, make the fringe by joining yarn between the last 2 hdc from Row 1, ch 1 (= 1st sc) and continue by working 49 sc between the hdc.

Note: The "rib" covers this row a little, so feel free to push the sts a bit with the left middle finger (for right-handers).

Cut yarn.

FINISHING

Back Seam

Fold the band in half, insert hook in the 1st st (that forms the "rib") and in the last st (also a "rib"), and put hook back in the loop with the marker, pull the loop through the 2 sts, ch 1 (= 1st sc), continue in sc over the next 22 sts, inserting hook through the 2 thicknesses. DO NOT WORK THE LAST 2 STS AT THE POINT.
Cut yarn.

STITCHES AND TECHNIQUES

• Magic circle, chain stitch, slip stitch, single crochet, double crochet, double crochet increase: **see Stitches, page 34.**
• Changing colors, pom-poms: **see Techniques, page 39.**

Note: Replace the 1st dc with ch 3 and pm in the 3rd ch (not indicated in pattern instructions).

SUPPLIES

• Bergère de France Idéal yarn (#3 light weight; 30% acrylic, 30% polyamide, 40% combed wool; 136 yd/124 m per 1.8 oz/50 g) in Sequoia (mahogany) or Persan (blue)
• Bergère de France Abakan yarn (#5 bulky weight; 68% polyamide, 32% polyester; 46 yd/42 m per 1.8 oz/50 g) in Ecru (white), or Bergère de France Teddy yarn (#4 medium weight; 100% polyamide; 87 yd/79.5 m per 1.8 oz/50 g) in Mastic (beige)
• 3.5 mm (US E-4) (for bonnet) and 6.0 mm (US J-10) (for edging) hooks

STITCHES AND TECHNIQUES

• Chain stitch, single crochet, half double crochet, working into the back loop only: **see Stitches, page 34.**
• Fringe: **see Techniques, page 39.**

SUPPLIES

FOR MARGUERITE

· Bergère de France Coton Fifty yarn (#2 fine weight; 4 ply; 50% cotton, 50% acrylic; 153 yd/140 m per 1.8 oz/50 g) in Berlingot (pink) and Coco (white)
· 1 small button
· 3.5 mm (US E-4) hook

STITCHES AND TECHNIQUES

· Magic circle, chain stitch, slip stitch, single crochet, double crochet, front and back post double crochet, single crochet bobble st: **see Stitches, page 34.**
· **Increase:** 1 dc AND 1 front post dc around the same st.

Note: Replace the 1st dc with ch 3 and pm in the 3rd ch (not indicated in pattern instructions).

Ties

Using 16 in/40 cm long strands of yarn, attach a fringe with 2 strands of Idéal yarn about 8 in/20 cm long as you would a fringe in each corner of the bonnet.

Cut a third strand of yarn about 11 in/30 cm long, and attach to the 2nd tie by tying a knot and leaving 3 in/8 cm on one end to weave in. For the 1st tie, use the tail left at the beginning for the 3rd strand.

Braid each side and finish with a slipknot.

Trim bottom of strands to even out.

DOTTED BONNET

INSTRUCTIONS

The number between parentheses is the number of sts at the end of the rnd (or row).

In pink, start with a magic circle.

Rnd 1: 12 dc, 1 sl st at the marker. (12 sts)

Rnd 2: Repeat 6 times *1 dc, 1 inc (work increase as "1 dc and 1 front post dc around the same st" here and throughout)*, 1 sl st at the marker. (18 sts)

Rnd 3: Repeat 6 times *2 dc, 1 inc*, 1 sl st at the marker. (24 sts)

Rnd 4: Repeat 6 times *3 dc, 1 inc*, 1 sl st at the marker. (30 sts)

Rnd 5: Repeat 6 times *4 dc, 1 inc*, 1 sl st at the marker. (36 sts)

Rnd 6: Repeat 6 times *5 dc, 1 inc*, 1 sl st at the marker. (42 sts)

Rnd 7: Repeat 6 times *6 dc, 1 inc*, 1 sl st at the marker. (48 sts)

Row 8: Repeat 5 times *7 dc, 1 inc*, DO NOT WORK THE REMAINING STS. (45 sts)

Row 9: Turn, 45 dc (with back post dc on the front post dc from the previous rnd). (45 sts)

Row 10: Turn, 45 dc (with front post dc on the back post dc from the previous rnd). (45 sts)

Row 11: Repeat Rnd 9.

Row 12: Repeat Rnd 10, and then make the tab closure as follows: ch 9, 1 sc in the 2nd ch from hook, 7 sc, 1 sl st in the last dc.

Row 13: Ch 1 (turning ch), repeat 14 times *[1 sc, ch 3 and 1 sl st in the sc] (= picot), 2 sl st, * 1 picot, ch 2 (= buttonhole), 1 sc.

Cut yarn.

FINISHING

Sew the small button on the last sc of the tab closure. To fasten the closure, slide the button between the 2 ch sts forming the buttonhole.

For a splash of fun, why not add some mini pom-poms?

Note: Be sure to leave enough yarn at the beginning and end to attach them onto the bonnet.

In white, crochet bobbles, attaching them to the bonnet by inserting hook on the wrong side around the post of a dc. When complete, tie 2 tight knots to secure and weave in ends.

POM-POM CAP

INSTRUCTIONS

The number between parentheses is the number of sts at the end of the row.
In black, begin by chaining 29 sts.
Row 1: 1 sc in the 2nd ch from hook, 27 sc. (28 sts)
Rows 2-40: Ch 1 to turn, 28 sc. (28 sts)
Row 41: Ch 1 to turn, 15 sc, DO NOT WORK THE REMAINING STS. (15 sts)
Rows 42-59: Ch 1 to turn, 15 sc. (15 sts)
Cut yarn.

FINISHING

Use whipstitch to sew the 15 sts to the top 15 sts on the other edge to form a tube.
Flatten and close the top of the cap.
Prepare 2 pom-poms, wrapping all the colors used together.
Attach pom-poms to the points.
For ties, sew 2 pieces of ribbon to the wrong side of the cap.

Note: You could chain stitch a tie to replace the ribbon.

BEANIE IN THREE VERSIONS:
DEER, BUNNY, AND BEAR CUB

INSTRUCTIONS

The number between parentheses is the number of sts at the end of the rnd (or row).

Basic Beanie
With brown (deer), beige (bunny), or mahogany (bear cub), begin by chaining 7 sts.
Rnd 1: 1 sc in the 2nd ch from hook (pm), 5 sc, go to other side of the chain, 6 sts. (12 sts)
Rnd 2: Repeat 6 times *1 sc, 1 inc*. (18 sts)
Rnd 3: Repeat 6 times *2 sc, 1 inc*. (24 sts)
Rnd 4: Repeat 6 times *3 sc, 1 inc*. (30 sts)
Rnd 5: Repeat 6 times *4 sc, 1 inc*. (36 sts)
Rnd 6: Repeat 6 times *5 sc, 1 inc*. (42 sts)
Rnd 7: Repeat 6 times *6 sc, 1 inc*. (48 sts)
Rnds 8-20: 48 sc. (48 sts)
Cut yarn.

SUPPLIES

FOR EMORY

· Bergère de France Coton Fifty yarn (#2 fine weight; 4 ply; 50% cotton, 50% acrylic; 153 yd/140 m per 1.8 oz/50 g) in Zan (black)
· Mercerized cotton (100% Egyptian cotton; 617 yd/565 m per 3.5 oz/100 g) in White (pom-poms)
· Ribbon or braid
· 3.5 mm (US E-4) hook

STITCHES AND TECHNIQUES

· Chain stitch, single crochet: **see Stitches, page 34.**
· Pom-poms, joining with whipstitch: **see Techniques, page 39.**

SUPPLIES

· Bergère de France Idéal yarn (#3 light weight; 30% acrylic, 30% polyamide, 40% combed wool; 136 yd/124 m per 1.8 oz/50 g) in following colors:
Deer: Tabac (brown), Vannerie (beige)
Bunny: Vannerie (beige)
Bear Cub: Sequoia (mahogany), a bit of Beige Rose (dusty rose)
· 4 mm (US G-6) hook

FOR FAWNTINE   FOR JO   FOR ABBOTT

STITCHES AND TECHNIQUES

- Magic circle, chain stitch, slip stitch, single crochet, single crochet increase: **see Stitches, page 34.**
- Working around a foundation chain, working in a spiral, joining with whipstitch: **see Techniques, page 39.**

Note: Work all rnds in spiral unless otherwise indicated.

Deer Beanie

Antlers

With beige, start with a magic circle.
Rnd 1: Ch 1, 1 sc (pm), 5 sc. (6 sts)
Rnd 2 and following: 6 sc. (6 sts)
Crochet 2 large antlers 2½ in/6 cm long and two small antlers 1¼ in/3 cm long.
Use the end of the hook to shape the points.
Then sew each small antler to one of the large antlers, about 1 in/2.5 cm up from the bottom. (See photo.)
DO NOT STUFF THEM.

Ears

Note: This is worked from the tip to the base of the ear.

With brown, ch 2 sts.
Row 1: 2 sc in the 2nd ch. (2 sts)
Row 2: Ch 1 to turn, 2 inc. (4 sts)
Row 3: Ch 1 to turn, 1 inc, 2 sc, 1 inc. (6 sts)
Row 4: Ch 1 to turn, 1 inc, 4 sc, 1 inc. (8 sts)
Row 5: Ch 1 to turn, 1 inc, 6 sc, 1 inc. (10 sts)
Row 6: Ch 1 to turn, 10 sc. (10 sts)
Cut, leaving a long tail.
With the needle, bring the yarn through the sts from the last row, and then pull to gather.
Make another identical ear.

Finishing

Put the beanie on the doll, positioning it more toward the back (see photo).
Sew the antlers to the front at Rnds 11/12, spacing them about ½ in/1.5 cm apart.
Sew the ears to 2 sts near the outside edge of each antler.

Bunny Beanie

Ears

Note: This is worked from the tip to the base of the ear.

With beige, start with a magic circle.
Rnd 1: Ch 1, 1 sc (pm), 5 sc. (6 sts)
Rnd 2: Repeat 3 times *1 sc, 1 inc*. (9 sts)
Rnd 3: 9 sc. (9 sts)
Rnd 4: Repeat 3 times *2 sc, 1 inc*. (12 sts)
Rnd 5: Repeat 3 times *3 sc, 1 inc*. (15 sts)
Rnd 6: Repeat 3 times *4 sc, 1 inc*. (18 sts)
Rnd 7: Repeat 3 times *5 sc, 1 inc*. (21 sts)
Rnds 8–17: 21 sc. (21 sts)
Row 18: Ch 1, and then join edges together with sl sts.
Cut yarn, leaving a long tail for sewing.
Make another identical ear.

Finishing

Fold the ear in half vertically. With the needle and the yarn tail, sew the ends of the ear together.

Note: Insert needle in the sc and not the sl sts so it holds better.

Put the cap on the doll, positioning it more toward the back (see photo).

Still using the same yarn, attach the ears, beginning between Rnds 4 and 5. *(Note: Counting from the outside edge, this would be Rnds 12 and 13.)* Bring the yarn under 2 sc from the same rnd (due to the thickness from joining edges), and then repeat 2 times *insert the needle into the edge of the ear again a bit farther down, bring the yarn under 2 sc from 1 rnd farther back*.

Bear Cub Beanie

Outer Ear

Note: This is worked from the top to the base of the ear.

With mahogany, start with a magic circle.
Rnd 1: Ch 1, 6 sc. (6 sts)
Rnd 2: 6 inc. (12 sts)
Rnd 3: Repeat 6 times *1 sc, 1 inc*. (18 sts)
Rnds 4-17: 18 sc. (18 sts)
Then ch 1, remove the hook and place colored marker in the loop. DO NOT CUT YARN.
Make another identical outer ear.

Inner Ear

With dusty rose, start with a magic circle.
Rnd 1: Ch 1, 6 sc, close with a sl st. (6 sts)
Rnd 2: 5 inc (= 10 sts). Do not join in the round; cut yarn, leaving a long tail for sewing.
Make another identical inner ear.

Finishing

Lay the outer ear flat so that the colored marker is on one side, and then attach inner ear with whipstitch, starting by inserting the needle in the last row of the ear and leaving 2 sts on the right edge.

Note: It is easier to assemble before closing the opening so the knot can go on the reverse side.

Replace the hook back in the loop of mahogany yarn and join edge to edge with sl sts, keeping the dusty rose part in the center. Hide the 3 yarn tails inside.

Do the same for the second ear.

Put the cap on the doll, positioning it more toward the back (see photo).
Attach ears with whipstitch between Rnds 7 and 8 (where there is 1 inc), going down the sides at an angle 1 rnd lower.
Space the ears 8 sts apart on the top of the head.

TIP

If the inner ear is not centered on the mahogany ear, work sl sts to help position it correctly.

SUPPLIES

· Bergère de France Coton Fifty yarn (#2 fine weight; 4 ply; 50% cotton, 50% acrylic; 153 yd/140 m per 1.8 oz/50 g) in Cytise (yellow) and Berlingot (pink)
· Bergère de France Metalika yarn (38% polyamide, 62% metal-effect polyester; 710 yd/649 m per 0.9 oz/25.5 g) in Libellule (silver) (optional, to bring some sparkle)
· White elastic
· 3 mm (US C-2 or D-3) hook

FOR LOLY

STITCHES AND TECHNIQUES

· Magic circle, chain stitch, single crochet, back loop only stitches, single crochet increase: **see Stitches, page 34.**
· Working in a spiral, pom-poms: **see Techniques, page 39.**

Note: Pm on the 1st sc of each rnd.

PARTY HAT

INSTRUCTIONS

The number between parentheses is the number of sts at the end of the rnd.
With yellow, start with a magic circle.
Rnd 1: Ch 1, 1 sc (pm), 4 sc. (5 sts)
Rnd 2: Repeat 2 times *1 sc, 1 inc*, 1 sc. (7 sts)
Rnd 3: Repeat 2 times *2 sc, 1 inc*, 1 sc. (9 sts)
Rnd 4: Repeat 2 times *3 sc, 1 inc*, 1 sc. (11 sts)
Rnd 5: Repeat 2 times *4 sc, 1 inc*, 1 sc. (13 sts)
Rnd 6: Repeat 2 times *5 sc, 1 inc*, 1 sc. (15 sts)
Continue to add 2 inc every rnd following the above pattern.
Rnd 23: Repeat 2 times *22 sc, 1 inc*, 1 sc. (49 sts)
Rnd 24: 12 sc, 1 inc, 23 sc, 1 inc, 12 sc. (51 sts)
✓ Place colored marker on the 2nd inc (for placement of elastic).
Rnd 25: 51 sc into back loop only. Cut yarn.
✓ Place colored marker on front loop of the 1st sc.
Rnd 26: (With pink and silver), 1 sc at the marker, ch 3, repeat 50 times *1 sc, ch 3*, working the sc in the unworked front loops of the sts from Rnd 24.
Cut yarn.

FINISHING

Prepare a pom-pom with all the colors together and attach to top of the hat, bringing the 2 yarn tails of the pom-pom through Rnd 1. Turn the hat over and tie 2 tight knots.
Attach the doubled piece of elastic at the colored markers, adjusting the length on the doll.

TOP HAT

INSTRUCTIONS

The number between parentheses is the number of sts at the end of the rnd.

Note: Crochet with dark blue (or white) unless otherwise indicated.

With dark blue (or white), start with a magic circle.
Rnd 1: Ch 1 (edge st), 6 sc. (6 sts)
Rnd 2: 6 inc. (12 sts)
Rnd 3: Repeat 6 times *1 sc, 1 inc*. (18 sts)
Rnd 4: Repeat 6 times *2 sc, 1 inc*. (24 sts)
Rnd 5: Repeat 6 times *3 sc, 1 inc*. (30 sts)
Rnd 6: Repeat 6 times *4 sc, 1 inc*. (36 sts)
Rnd 7: Repeat 6 times *5 sc, 1 inc*. (42 sts)
Rnd 8: Repeat 6 times *6 sc, 1 inc*. (48 sts)
Rnd 9: 48 sc into back loop only. (48 sts)

SUPPLIES

· Bergère de France Coton Fifty yarn (#2 fine weight; 4 ply; 50% cotton, 50% acrylic; 153 yd/140 m per 1.8 oz/50 g) in the following colors:
Version A: Petrolier (dark blue), Nectarine (coral)
Version B: Coco (white), Bengale (fuchsia)
· White elastic
· 3 mm (US C-2 or D-3) hook (or larger for a larger hat)

FOR GRETA

FOR ROSIE

Rnd 10: 48 sc. (48 sts)
Rnd 11 (coral or fuchsia): 48 sc. (48 sts)
Rnds 12-13: 48 sc. (48 sts)
Rnd 14 (coral or fuchsia): 48 sc. (48 sts)
Rnds 15-16: 48 sc. (48 sts)
Rnd 17: Repeat 12 times *3 sc, 1 dot*. (48 sts)
Rnd 18: 48 sc. (48 sts)
Rnd 19: 2 sc, repeat 11 times *1 dot, 3 sc*, 1 dot, 1 sc. (48 sts)
Rnd 20: 48 sc. (48 sts)
Rnd 21: Repeat 12 times *1 dot, 3 sc*. (48 sts)
Rnd 22: 48 sc. (48 sts)
Cut dark blue (or white) yarn, leaving enough tail to weave in.
Rnd 23 (coral or fuchsia): Repeat 24 times *1 sc, 1 inc* working into front loops only. (72 sts)
✓ Place colored marker on the back unworked loop of the 18th and 54th sts.
Rnds 24-26 (coral or fuchsia): 72 sc. (72 sts)
Rnd 27 (dark blue or white): Repeat 9 times *7 sc, 1 inc*, sl st in the 1st sc. (81 sts)
Cut yarn.
Attach the elastic thread at the markers, adjusting length on the doll.

HAIR

FRIZZY PIGTAILS

INSTRUCTIONS

The number between parentheses is the number of sts at the end of the rnd.

Basic Hair Cap
Start with a magic circle.
Rnd 1: 12 dc, sl st at the marker. (12 sts)
Rnd 2: 12 inc, sl st at the marker. (24 sts)
Rnd 3: Repeat 6 times *3 dc, 1 inc*, sl st at the marker. (30 sts)
Rnd 4: 30 dc, sl st at the marker. (30 sts)
Rnd 5: 13 dc, 1 hdc, 1 sc, 1 sl st, 1 sc, 1 hdc, 12 dc, 1 sl st at the marker. (30 sts)
Cut yarn (= center back of the head).

STITCHES AND TECHNIQUES
· Magic circle, chain stitch, single crochet, single crochet increase, back loop only stitches: **see Stitches, page 34.**
· Working in a spiral, changing colors: **see Techniques, page 39.**
· **Dots** (in coral or fuchsia): Insert hook in the st, pull through coral (or fuchsia) yarn. There are 2 loops on the hook: 1 blue (or white), 1 coral (or fuchsia). Yarn over with the blue (or white) yarn and pull through the 2 loops. Visually, the top "V" of the sts (seen from above) are all blue (or white). Stitch over the blue and coral (or white and fuchsia) yarns to hide them.

SUPPLIES
· Bergère de France Teddy yarn (#4 medium weight; 100% polyamide; 87 yd/79.5 m per 1.8 oz/50 g) in Mastic (beige)
· 5 mm (US H-8) hook

FOR GRETA

FOR ROSIE

STITCHES AND TECHNIQUES

- Magic circle, chain stitch, slip stitch, single crochet, half double crochet, double crochet, double crochet increase: **see Stitches, page 34.**
- Tassels: **see Techniques, page 39.**

Notes: Replace the 1st dc with ch 3 and pm in the 3rd ch of each rnd (not indicated in pattern instructions).

With this yarn it is difficult to see the sts (as well as any mistakes, luckily!). To distinguish the top "V" of the dc, start from the post of the st and go up.

SUPPLIES

- Bergère de France Idéal yarn (#3 light weight; 30% acrylic, 30% polyamide, 40% combed wool; 136 yd/124 m per 1.8 oz/50 g) in the following colors:

Large bun: Tabac (brown)
Long hair: Vannerie (beige), Beige Rose (dusty rose)
Short pigtails: Vannerie (beige), Tabac (brown)

- 6 mm (US J-10) hook

FOR SALOMÉ   FOR LOLY   FOR TINA

FOR SOPHIA   FOR HYACINTH & ROSEMARY

Pigtails

Make a tassel using a 2⅜–2¾ in/6–7 cm piece of cardboard. Using the 2 strands of yarn, attach the pigtail to the basic hair at the desired height, sliding yarn through each side of a dc. Tie 2 knots on wrong side and weave in ends. Make another identical tassle and attach it to opposite side in same way.

LARGE BUN, LONG HAIR, OR SHORT PIGTAILS

INSTRUCTIONS

The number between parentheses is the number of sts at the end of the rnd (or row).

Basic Hair Cap for All 3 Versions

In desired color, and using 2 strands of yarn, start with a magic circle.
Rnd 1: Ch 1, 6 sc. (6 sts)
Rnd 2: 6 inc. (12 sts)
Rnd 3: Repeat 6 times *1 sc, 1 inc*. (18 sts)
Rnd 4: Repeat 6 times *2 sc, 1 inc*. (24 sts)
Rnd 5: Repeat 6 times *3 sc, 1 inc*. (30 sts)
Rnd 6: Repeat 6 times *4 sc, 1 inc*. (36 sts)
Rnds 7-11: 36 sc. (36 sts) DO NOT CUT YARN.

Large Bun

Finishing the Basic Hair

Rnd 12: 1 sc, repeat 2 times *skip 1 st, 5 sc in the same st, skip 1 st, 1 sl st* (= bangs), skip 1 st, 5 sc in the same st, skip 1 st, 25 sc. (Note: The last sc is on the 1st sc of Rnd 11.)
Row 13: Ch 1 to turn, sc2tog, 21 sc, sc2tog. (23 sts) Do not work the remaining sts.
Row 14: Ch 1 to turn, sc2tog, 19 sc, sc2tog. (21 sts) Cut yarn.

Bun

To make the bun, again work Rnds 1–3 of the basic hair cap, and then:

Rnds 4-6: 18 sc. (18 sts)

Cut yarn and leave a long tail for sewing.

Stuff the bun a bit. With the needle, join together using whipstitch between Rnds 2 and 3 of the basic hair cap.

Personalize by adding a fabric bow or ribbon to go around the bun.

✓ **Fabric hair ribbon:** With a decorative ribbon about 8 in/ 20 cm long, tie a pretty bow around the bun, and then cut ends off evenly.

Long Hair

Finishing the Basic Hair

Rnd 12: 5 sc, repeat 15 times *1 sc, ch 4, sl st in the 2nd ch from hook, sl st in each of the next 2 ch sts* (= bangs), 16 sc. (36 sts)

Row 13: 6 sc, ch 9, sl st in the 2nd ch from hook, sl st in each of the next 7 ch sts, turn work *(Note: Don't work the bangs sts)*, 1 sc, ch 9, sl st in the 2nd ch from hook, sl st in each of the next 7 ch sts, repeat 20 times *1 sc, ch 8, sl st in the 2nd ch from hook, sl st in each of the next 6 ch sts*. Repeat 2 times **1 sc, ch 9, sl st in the 2nd ch from hook, sl st in each of the next 7 ch sts**.

Cut yarn.

Short Pigtails

Finishing the Basic Hair

Rnd 12: [3 sc, 3 hdc, 3 dc, 3 tr, 3 ch st, 1 sl st in the next st] (= bangs), 23 sc. (35 sts)

Rnd 13: 12 sc, 1 sc in the 3rd ch st of the previous rnd, ch 4, 1 sl sp in the next st, 1 sl st (colored marker), 20 sc, 1 sl st. (36 sts)

Row 14: Ch 1 to turn, DO NOT WORK INTO THE SL ST FROM THE PREVIOUS RND, 4 sc, ch 3, 1 sl st in the next st. DO NOT CUT YARN.

First pigtail: Repeat 8 times *ch 12, turn, 1 sl st into the ch-3 space*. Cut yarn.

Join yarns at colored marker then: 1 sc, ch 3, 1 sl st in the next st. DO NOT CUT YARN and make the **second pigtail**: Repeat 8 times *ch 12, turn, 1 sl st in the ch-3 space*. Cut yarn. Tie a decorative ribbon, cord or some yarn around each pigtail.

STITCHES AND TECHNIQUES

• Magic circle, chain stitch, slip stitch, single crochet, single crochet increase or decrease, half double crochet, double crochet, triple crochet: **see Stitches, page 34.**

• Working in a spiral, joining with whipstitch: **see Techniques, page 39.**

Note: All versions are worked with 2 strands of yarn held together (for the single-color version—the large bun—use the 2 ends of the same ball of yarn).

Work rnds in spiral and pm on the 1st sc of rnd (not included in pattern instructions).

SUPPLIES

- **For Braids:** Bergère de France Baltic yarn (#5 bulky weight; 40% polyamide, 60% acrylic; 87 yd/79.5 m per 1.8 oz/50 g) in Roux Poudré (frosted rust)
- **For Double Buns:** Bergère de France Baltic yarn (#5 bulky weight; 40% polyamide, 60% acrylic; 87 yd/79.5 m per 1.8 oz/50 g) in Ecru; Bergère de France Metalika yarn (38% polyamide, 62% metal-effect polyester; 710 yd/649 m per 0.9 oz/25.5 g) in Etoile (gold)

  Note: The Metalika yarn is optional and doesn't change proportions; it just brings some small, sunlit strands!
- Ribbon (optional, for hair ties)
- 5 mm (H-8) hook

FOR PIA   FOR DOMI   FOR DINA   FOR PIKI

STITCHES AND TECHNIQUES

- Magic circle, slip stitch, single crochet, half double crochet, double crochet, double crochet increase: **see Stitches, page 34.**
- Fringe, joining with whipstitch: **see Techniques, page 39.**

Notes: Replace the 1st dc with ch 3 and pm in the 3rd ch of each rnd.

SUPPLIES

- Bergère de France Coton Fifty yarn (#2 fine weight; 4 ply; 50% cotton, 50% acrylic; 153 yd/140 m per 1.8 oz/50 g) in Zan (black)
- 3.5 mm (US E-4) hook

BRAIDS OR DOUBLE BUNS

INSTRUCTIONS

The number between parentheses is the number of sts at the end of the rnd.

Basic Hair Cap for All Versions
Start with a magic circle.
Rnd 1: 12 dc, sl st at the marker. (12 sts)
Rnd 2: 12 inc, sl st at the marker. (24 sts)
Rnd 3: Repeat 6 times *3 dc, 1 inc*, sl st at the marker. (30 sts)
Rnd 4: 30 dc, sl st at the marker. (30 sts)
Rnd 5: 13 dc, 1 hdc, 1 sc, 1 sl st, 1 sc, 1 hdc, 12 dc, sl st at the marker. (30 sts)
Rnd 6: Repeat Rnd 5.
Cut yarn (= center back of head).
✓ **For braids:** Place 4 colored markers on 4th, 9th, 23rd, and 27th sts.

Braids
Cut 12 strands of yarn about 10½ in/27 cm long.
Attach a fringe of 2 strands at each of the 2 markers on one side and on the 4 sts in between these markers.
Make a braid with these 12 strands (dividing them intro groups of 4 strands each).
At ¾ in/2 cm from the end, with a short length of yarn, tie off the braid with 2 tight knots.
Wrap a small ribbon around (optional) and make a pretty bow.
Even up the ends with scissors.
Repeat for the second braid at the other 2 markers.

Double Bun
Start with a magic circle.
Rnd 1: 12 dc, sl st at the marker. (12 sts)
Rnds 2-3: 12 dc, sl st at the marker. (12 sts)
Cut yarn, leaving a long tail for sewing. Stuff lightly.
Place the base hair on the doll, position a bun on the side at Rnds 4 and 5 and sew on with whipstitch.
Repeat for the second bun and attach it to the opposite side.
Put the wig on the head, placing it more toward the back (see photo).

SQUARE CUT

INSTRUCTIONS

The number between parentheses is the number of sts at the end of the rnd (or row).

Oval Hair Cap
Chain 7 sts for foundation chain and work around it in a spiral.

Rnd 1: 1 sc in the 2nd ch from hook (pm), 5 sc, go to other side of the chain, 6 sts. (12 sts)
Rnd 2: Repeat 6 times *1 sc, 1 inc*. (18 sts)
Rnd 3: Repeat 6 times *2 sc, 1 inc*. (24 sts)
Rnd 4: Repeat 6 times *3 sc, 1 inc*, sl st at the marker and leave it in place. (30 sts) DO NOT CUT YARN.

"Vertical" Part

Row 1: Ch 21.
Row 2: 1 sc in the 2nd ch from hook, 19 sc, sl st at the marker. (20 sts)
Row 3: Ch 1 to turn, 20 sc into back loop only. (20 sts) BE SURE NOT TO WORK SL ST AT THE BEGINNING OF THE RND.
Row 4: Ch 1 to turn, 20 sc into back loop only (BLO), sl st in next st of the oval hair cap.
Rows 5-6: Repeat Rows 3 and 4.
Row 7: Ch 1 to turn, 9 sc into BLO. (9 sts) DO NOT WORK REMAINING STITCHES.
Row 8: Ch 1 to turn, 9 sc into BLO, sl st in next st of oval base.
Rows 9-32: Repeat Rows 7 and 8 twelve times.
Row 33: Ch 1 to turn, 9 sc into BLO, ch 12.
Row 34: 1 sc in the 2nd ch from hook, 11 sc in the chain, 9 sc into BLO, sl st in next st of oval base.
Row 35: Ch 1 to turn, 20 sc into BLO. (20 sts)
Row 36: Ch 1 to turn, 20 sc into BLO, sl st in next st of oval base.
Rows 37-60: Repeat Rows 35 and 36 twelve times.
Row 61: Ch 1 to turn, 20 sc into BLO. (20 sts) DO NOT CUT YARN.

ASSEMBLY

Ch 1, work 20 sc, inserting the hook each time in the last st of Row 61 and Row 1 at the same time. Cut yarn.

CURLY HAIR

INSTRUCTIONS

The number between parentheses is the number of sts at the end of the rnd.
Start with a magic circle.
Rnd 1: Ch 1, 6 sc. (6 sts)
Rnd 2: Work 6 inc in loop st. (12 sts)
Rnd 3: Repeat 6 times *1 sc, 1 inc*. (18 sts)
Rnd 4: Repeat 6 times *2 sc, 1 inc* in loop st. (24 sts)
Rnd 5: Repeat 6 times *3 sc, 1 inc*. (30 sts)
Rnd 6: Repeat 6 times *4 sc, 1 inc* in loop st. (36 sts)
Rnd 7: Repeat 6 times *5 sc, 1 inc*. (42 sts)
Rnd 8: 42 sc in loop st. (42 sts)
Rnd 9: 42 sc. (42 sts)
Rnds 10-14: Repeat Rnds 8 and 9.

STITCHES AND TECHNIQUES

· Chain stitch, slip stitch, single crochet, single crochet increase, back loop only stitches: **see Stitches, page 34.**
· Working around a chain, working in a spiral: **see Techniques, page 39.**

Note: Unless otherwise indicated, work rnds in spiral and pm on the 1st st of each rnd.

FOR ANNA

FOR NINA

SUPPLIES

· Bergère de France Idéal yarn (#3 light weight; 30% acrylic, 30% polyamide, 40% combed wool; 136 yd/124 m per 1.8 oz/50 g) in Vannerie (beige)
· 3.5 mm (US E-4) hook
· Ruler or rod (for the loop stitch)

FOR MARY-SUN   FOR JOSETTE

STITCHES AND TECHNIQUES

· Magic circle, chain stitch, single crochet, single crochet increase: **see Stitches, page 34.**

· **Loop stitch with small loops:** *(Note: Made using the middle finger)* Repeat *insert hook in the st, loop yarn over left middle finger, bring hook over the front leg of the loop and then pull the two strands at the base of the loop through the stitch (now 3 loops on the hook), yo and pull through the 3 loops and remove finger from loop*.

· **Loop stitch with large loops:** *(Note: Made using a ruler, to be held behind the work)* Repeat *insert hook in the st, loop yarn over the ruler (from front to back), bring hook over the front leg of the loop and then pull the two strands at the base of the loop through the stitch (now 3 loops on the hook), yo and pull through the 3 loops*. Leave loop on the ruler and repeat for a dozen sts, and then remove ruler from loops. The loops are formed on the back side.

· Working in a spiral: **see Techniques, page 39.**

Notes: The loop st is a variation of the sc. Pm on the 1st sc of each rnd.

Sequence of stitches: Alternate 1 rnd of "classic" sc and 1 rnd of loop stitch, except at Rnd 15.

SUPPLIES

· Bergère de France Coton Fifty yarn (#2 fine weight; 4 ply; 50% cotton, 50% acrylic; 153 yd/140 m per 1.8 oz/50 g) in Coquille (peach beige)
· Bergère de France Angel 50 yarn (#2 fine weight; 24% mohair, 32% acrylic, 44% polyamide; 601 yd/549.5 m per 1.8 oz/50g) in Blanc Cassé (off-white)
· Ribbon
· 4 mm (US G-6) hook

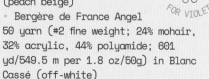

FOR VIOLET

Put the wig on the doll (centered at the top of the head) and check whether the height is right (= height of bangs).
Rnd 15: 30 sc in loop st. (30 sts) DO NOT WORK THE REST OF THE STS, which correspond to the front bangs.
Rnd 16: Ch 1 to turn, 30 sc. (30 sts)
Rnd 17: Ch 1 to turn, 30 sc in loop st. (30 sts)
Rnds 18–21: Repeat Rnds 16 and 17. Cut yarn.

LONG PRINCESS HAIR

INSTRUCTIONS

The number between parentheses is the number of sts at the end of the rnd.

Base

Start with a magic circle.

Rnd 1: 12 dc, sl st at the marker. (12 sts)
Rnd 2: 12 inc, sl st at the marker. (24 sts)
Rnd 3: Repeat 12 times *1 dc, 1 inc*, sl st at the marker. (36 sts)
Rnds 4–7: 36 dc. (36 sts) DO NOT CUT YARN.

Bangs

Rnd 8: Ch 1 (edge st), 17 sc into back loop only. (17 sts)
Rnd 9: Ch 1 to turn the work, 17 sc. (17 sts)
Rnd 10: Ch 1 to turn, sc2tog, 13 sc, sc2tog. (15 sts)
Rnd 11: Ch 1 to turn, skip the 1st st, 13 sc, sl st in the last st.
Cut yarn.

FINISHING

With both yarns held together, cut strands to the desired length.
Make fringe from 4 strands (2 of each yarn), attaching to the front loop of the Rnd 7 sts.
Put the hair on the doll's head, more toward the back (see photo). Comb through strands with fingers a bit to smooth. With the doll's head facing down, gather all the strands of yarn together to form a high ponytail. Don't pull too tightly, so that it puffs up some over the base. Slide a small rubber band or tie a piece of yarn around it. Add pom-poms, a ribbon, etc.

–
OUTERWEAR
–

FURRY SHEPHERD'S VEST AND CARDIGAN

INSTRUCTIONS

The number between parentheses is the number of sts at the end of the row.

Body for Both Versions

Bottom

With Teddy and with 5 mm (US H-8) hook, chain 31 sts.
Row 1: 1 dc in the 5th ch (pm), 26 dc. (28 sts)
Row 2: 6 dc, dc2tog, 12 dc, dc2tog, 6 dc. (26 sts)
Row 3: 6 dc, dc2tog, 10 dc, dc2tog, 6 dc. (24 sts)

STITCHES AND TECHNIQUES

· Magic circle, chain stitch, slip stitch, single crochet, back loop only stitches, double crochet, double crochet increase, single crochet 2 together: **see Stitches, page 34.**
· Fringe, pom-poms: **see Techniques, page 39.**

Notes: Replace the 1st dc with ch 3 and pm in the 3rd ch of each rnd.

Crochet entire pattern with one strand of each yarn held together.

SUPPLIES

· **Shepherd's Vest:** Bergère de France Teddy yarn (#4 medium weight; 100% polyamide; 87 yd/79.5 m per 1.8 oz/50 g) in Mastic (beige); Bergère de France Idéal yarn (#3 light weight; 30% acrylic, 30% polyamide, 40% combed wool; 136 yd/124 m per 1.8 oz/50 g) in Girolle (mustard)

· **Cardigan:** Bergère de France Teddy yarn (#4 medium weight; 100% polyamide; 87 yd/79.5 m per 1.8 oz/50 g) in Fard (pale pink); Bergère de France Idéal yarn (#3 light weight; 30% acrylic, 30% polyamide, 40% combed wool; 136 yd/124 m per 1.8 oz/50 g) in Cendre (gray)

· 4 mm (US G-6) and 5 mm (US H-8) hooks

FOR TINA

FOR AVERY

65

STITCHES AND TECHNIQUES

• Chain stitch, slip stitch, single crochet, working in the back loop only, double crochet, double crochet 2 together: **see Stitches, page 34.**

• Working in a spiral, joining in whipstitch, changing colors: **see Techniques, page 39.**

Notes: With the Teddy yarn it is difficult to see the sts (as well as any mistakes, luckily!). To distinguish the top "V" of the dc, start from the post of the st and go up.

Replace the 1st dc with ch 3 and pm in the 3rd ch (except for Row 1).

Row 4: 5 dc, dc2tog, 10 dc, dc2tog, 5 dc. (22 sts)

✓ **For the vest,** place 1 colored marker on the first and last dc of this row (= placement of **ties**).

Front Left Side

Row 5: 1 dc, skip 1 st, 3 dc. (4 sts) DO NOT WORK REMAINING STS.

Row 6: 2 dc, dc2tog. (3 sts)

Cut yarn, leaving 6 in/15 cm of yarn tail for the seam.

Front Right Side

Attach yarn to the last st of Row 4, repeat Rows 5 and 6.

Back

Attach yarn to the 3rd st of Row 4 (= skip 2 sts after a front side for the underarm).

Rows 5-6: 8 dc. (8 sts) DO NOT WORK THE LAST 2 STS BEFORE THE 2nd FRONT SIDE (for the underarm).

For the **shoulders**, seam the 3 sts of each front side to the corresponding 3 sts on the back.

For the Vest

Edging around Body and Armholes

In Idéal with 4 mm (US G-6) hook, attach yarn to the last st on the bottom, work sc all the way around the bottom, go up the front opening, working into 1 loop on the side of dc sts, and then continue around the neckline and go down the other side of the front, closing with a sl st in the 1st sc. Cut yarn.

Do the same for the armholes.

Ties

In Idéal with 4 mm (US G-6) hook, attach yarn to the edging sc next to the colored marker, ch 25 (or more for a longer tie), 1 sl st in the 2nd ch from hook, 24 sl sts, 1 sl st in the starting sc. Cut yarn.

Repeat steps at the second marker for the other tie.

For the Cardigan

Sleeves

Attach Teddy yarn at underarm on the right side of the work, and then crochet (inserting hook around edge of armhole in Rnd 1):

Rnds 1-4: 9 dc, 1 sl st in the 3rd ch st. (9 sts)

Switch to Idéal yarn at the last sl st and finish with 4 mm (US G-6) hook.

Rnd 5: Ch 1, 1 sc (pm), 8 sc. (9 sts) Continue in spiral directly at the marker.

Rnd 6: 9 sc in back loop only. (9 sts)

Cut yarn.

Repeat steps for other sleeve.

Edging

In Idéal with 4 mm (G-6) hook, attach yarn to the last st on the bottom, on right side of work, and sc along lower edge of cardigan. Fasten off with a sl st. Cut yarn.

Pockets

In Idéal with 4 mm (US G-6) hook, chain 10 sts.

Row 1: 1 dc in the 5th ch, 5 dc. (7 sts)

Row 2: Ch 3 (= 1st dc), 6 dc (= 7 sts) and cut yarn, leaving 6 in/15 cm tail for sewing.

Make another identical pocket.

Attach pockets to front sides using whipstitch, sewing the vertical sides of the pocket onto the cardigan at a width that is less than that of the pocket. This provides space to slip the doll's hands inside the pockets.

RETRO GRANNY JACKET

INSTRUCTIONS

Granny Square

In color 1, start with a magic circle.

Row 1: Ch 3 (pm in the 3rd ch st), 1 dc, repeat 3 times *ch 2, 3 dc*, ch 2, 1 dc, close with sl st at the marker, cut yarn.

Row 2: Join color 2 in a ch-2 space, [ch 3 (= 1st dc), 2 dc, ch 2, and 3 dc] in this same space, repeat 3 times *[3 dc, ch 2, and 3 dc] in next chain space*, sl st at the marker, cut yarn.

Key

◂ Cut yarn.

◁ Attach yarn.

◯ 1 magic circle

◦ **Chain 1:** Yo, pull through loop on the hook.

– **1 slip stitch:** Insert hook in st, yo and draw through all loops on hook.

 1 double crochet: Yo then insert hook in st, yo and pull through st, and then repeat *yo, pull through 2 loops*.

Granny Square

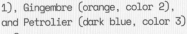

Half Granny Square

In color 1, start with a magic circle.

Row 1: Ch 3 (pm in the 3rd ch st), 3 dc, ch 2, 4 dc, cut yarn.

Row 2: Don't turn work but join color 2 at the marker, ch 3, 3 dc in same space, [3 dc, ch 2, 3 dc] in next ch-2 space, 4 dc in the last st; cut yarn.

Half Granny Square

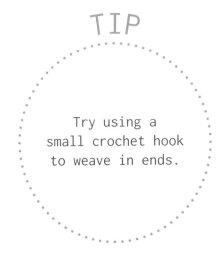

TIP

Try using a small crochet hook to weave in ends.

SUPPLIES

• Bergère de France Coton Fifty yarn (#2 fine weight; 4 ply; 50% cotton, 50% acrylic; 153 yd/140 m per 1.8 oz/50 g) in following colors: Zan (black, color 1), Gingembre (orange, color 2), and Petrolier (dark blue, color 3)

• 2 snaps

• 3 mm (US C-2 or D-3) hook

STITCHES AND TECHNIQUES

• Magic circle, chain stitch, slip stitch, double crochet: **see Stitches, page 34.**

• Joining with whipstitch: **see Techniques, page 39.**

Joining the Squares

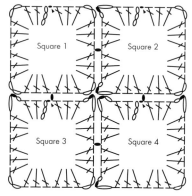

Placement of Squares

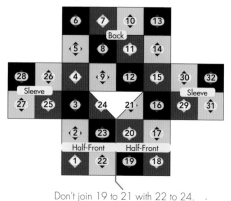

Don't join 19 to 21 with 22 to 24.

- ■ Black
- ▨ Orange
- ■ Dark blue

Join-As-You-Go Method

Start by crocheting 1 complete square; work Rnd 1 of a 2nd square and work Rnd 2 while joining it to the side of the 1st one as follows:

Rnd 2: Join the new color in a ch-2 space, [ch 3 (pm in the 3rd ch st), 2 dc] in this same space, ch 1, 1 sl st in the ch space corresponding to the 1st square (1st join made), ch 1, 3 dc in the same space, insert the hook on the side between the 2 groups of dc from the 1st square, 1 sl st (2nd join made), 3 dc in the next ch space, ch 1, insert hook in the 2nd ch space from the 1st square, 1 sl st (3rd join made), ch 1, repeat 2 times *3 dc, ch 2, 3 dc in the next ch space*, 1 sl st at the marker, cut yarn. Then continue following the same pattern for the following squares, as shown in the diagram to the left.

Crochet a total of 30 squares and 2 half squares:
- 11 squares and 1 half square in black and orange
- 9 squares and 1 half square in orange and blue
- 10 squares in blue and black

Then join as shown in the diagram.

FINISHING

Sew the sleeve underarm seam and the sides, sewing into the loops that are most to the outside:

Note: It is also possible to not join-as-you-go. In that case, crochet 30 squares and 2 half squares (positioning them in accordance with the diagram), and join them using the whipstitch.

Sew on snaps.

FUZZY FAUX FUR JACKET

INSTRUCTIONS

The number between parentheses is the number of sts at the end of the row (or rnd).

Bottom of the Body

Begin by chaining 51 sts.

Row 1: 1 dc in the 5th ch, 46 dc. (48 sts)

Row 2: DO NOT TURN WORK, repeat *5 ch st, 1 sl st in the FRONT loop of the next stitch*, starting with the 2nd dc and ending with a sl st in the last ch replacing the 1st dc. (47 ch spaces)

Row 3: (IN THE BACK LOOP ONLY OF THE STS IN NEXT TO LAST ROW), 11 dc, repeat 2 times *dc2tog, 10 dc*, dc2tog, 11 dc. (45 sts)

Row 4: Repeat Row 2. (44 ch spaces)

Row 5: 14 dc, dc2tog, 13 dc, dc2tog, 14 dc. (43 sts)

Row 6: Repeat Row 2. (42 ch spaces)

Row 7: 8 dc, repeat 2 times *dc2tog, 10 dc*, dc2tog, 9 dc. (40 sts)

Row 8: Repeat Row 2. (39 ch spaces)

Row 9: 6 dc, repeat 3 times *dc2tog, 7 dc*, dc2tog, 5 dc. (36 sts)

Row 10: Repeat Row 2. (35 ch spaces)

Row 11: 11 dc, dc2tog, 10 dc, dc2tog, 11 dc. (34 sts)

Row 12: Repeat Row 2. (33 ch spaces)

Row 13: 10 dc, dc2tog, 10 dc, dc2tog, 10 dc. (32 sts)

Row 14: Repeat Row 2. (31 ch spaces)

Row 15: 32 dc. (32 sts)

Row 16: Repeat Row 2. (31 ch spaces)

DO NOT CUT YARN

Front Right Side

Row 17: Dc2tog (= ch 2 and 1 dc), 5 dc. (6 sts)

Row 18: Repeat Row 2. (5 ch spaces)

Row 19: Dc2tog (= ch 2 and 1 dc), 4 dc. (5 sts)

Row 20: Repeat Row 2. (4 ch spaces)

Row 21: Dc2tog, 3 dc. (4 sts)

Row 22: Repeat Row 2. (3 ch spaces)

Cut yarn, leaving a long tail for sewing.

Back

Join yarn on the right side of the work at Row 16, skip 2 sts (place colored marker on the 2nd st for sleeve placement), and then:

Row 17: 15 dc. (15 sts)

Row 18: Repeat Row 2. (14 ch spaces)

Row 19: 15 dc. (15 sts)

Row 20: Repeat Row 2. (14 ch spaces)

Cut yarn.

SUPPLIES

· Bergère de France Coton Fifty yarn (#2 fine weight; 4 ply; 50% cotton, 50% acrylic; 153 yd/140 m per 1.8 oz/50 g) in Petrolier (dark blue)
· 3 mm (US C-2 or D-3) hook

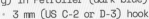

FOR GRETA

STITCHES AND TECHNIQUES

· Chain stitch, slip stitch, single crochet, double crochet, double crochet increase or decrease: **see Stitches, page 34.**
· Joining with whipstitch: **see Techniques, page 39.**

Note: Replace the 1st dc with ch 3 and pm in the 3rd ch of each row.

Front Left Side

Join yarn on the right side of the work at Row 16, skip 2 sts (place colored marker on the 2nd st for sleeve placement), and then:

Row 17: 5 dc, dc2tog. (6 sts)
Row 18: Repeat Row 2. (5 ch spaces)
Row 19: 4 dc, dc2tog. (5 sts)
Row 20: Repeat Row 2. (4 ch spaces)
Row 21: 3 dc, dc2tog. (4 sts)
Row 22: Repeat Row 2. (3 ch spaces)

Cut yarn, leaving a long tail for sewing.

FINISHING

With needle, join shoulders using whipstitch through the 4 back loops on each side.

Sleeves

On the right side of the work, attach yarn at the left underarm colored marker (there are 2 sts not worked), and then:

Rnd 1: Ch 3 (pm on the 3rd ch st), work on the side of the dc between each row of ch spaces. To do that, repeat 3 times *1 inc, 1 dc in the next st*, 1 dc at the 2nd st not worked, 1 sl st in the front loop at the marker, move marker to back loop. (11 sts)
Rnd 2: DON'T TURN WORK, repeat *5 ch sts, 1 sl st in the FRONT loop of each dc*, finish with 1 sl st in the back loop at the marker. (11 ch spaces)
Rnd 3: Ch 3 (pm on the 3rd ch st), 10 dc in the back loop of the dc from the next to last rnd. (11 sts)
Rnd 4: Repeat Rnd 2.
Rnds 5–16: Repeat Rnds 3 and 4.

Then finish in spiral (don't join the rnd with a sl st as previously), as follows:

Rnd 17: Ch 1, 1 sc (pm), 10 sc. (11 sts)
Rnds 18–19: 1 sc (pm), 10 sc in the front loop. (11 sts)

Finish with a sl st at the marker, fasten off with ch 1 and cut yarn.

Repeat these steps for the second sleeve (beginning at the colored marker on the right underarm).

CABLE TWIST CARDIGAN

INSTRUCTIONS

The number between parentheses is the number of sts at the end of the row.

Body

Note: Worked from the neckline down.

With white and gold held together, chain 30 sts.

SUPPLIES

• Bergère de France Idéal yarn (#3 light weight; 30% acrylic, 30% polyamide, 40% combed wool; 136 yd/124 m per 1.8 oz/50 g) in Girolle (mustard) and Everest (white)
• Bergère de France Metalika yarn (38% polyamide, 62% metal-effect polyester; 710 yd/649 m per 0.9 oz/25.5 g) in Etoile (gold) (optional)
• 4 small buttons
• 4 mm (US G-6) hook

FOR ABBOTT

Row 1: 1 sc in the 2nd ch, 28 sc. (29 sts) Switch to mustard on the last sc.

Row 2: Ch 1 to turn, 5 sc, 1 sc inc, 3 sc, 1 sc inc, 9 sc, 1 sc inc, 3 sc, 1 sc inc, 5 sc. (33 sts)

Row 3: 5 dc, 1 V, 5 dc, 1 V, 9 dc, 1 V, 5 dc, 1 V, 5 dc. (41 sts) Place colored marker on the V ch sts to locate them more easily.

Row 4 (RS): 2 dc, 1 front post dc (fpdc), 1 popcorn st, 1 fpdc, 2 dc, 1 V, 7 dc, 1 V, 13 dc, 1 V, 7 dc, 1 V, 2 dc, 1 fpdc, 1 popcorn st, 1 fpdc, 2 dc. (49 sts) Place 1 colored marker on the V ch sts.

Row 5 (divide for arms): 2 dc, 1 back post dc (bpdc), 1 dc, 1 bpdc, 3 dc, dc2tog by inserting hook under the 2 markers (skipping the 9 sts between markers for the 1st armhole), 15 dc, dc2tog by inserting hook under the 2 markers (= 2nd armhole), 3 dc, 1 bpdc, 1 dc, 1 bpdc, 2 dc. (33 sts) Leave the 4 colored markers (they will be used for the sleeves).

Row 6: 2 dc, 1 fpdc, 1 popcorn st, 1 fpdc, 23 dc, 1 fpdc, 1 popcorn st, 1 fpdc, 2 dc. (33 sts)

Row 7: 2 dc, 1 bpdc, 1 dc, 1 bpdc, 3 dc, 1 dc inc, 15 dc, 1 dc inc, 3 dc, 1 bpdc, 1 dc, 1 bpdc, 2 dc. (35 sts)

Row 8: 2 dc, 1 fpdc, 1 popcorn st, 1 fpdc, 1 dc, 1 dc inc, 10 dc, 1 dc inc, 10 dc, 1 dc inc, 1 dc, 1 fpdc, 1 popcorn st, 1 fpdc, 2 dc. (38 sts)

Row 9: 2 dc, 1 bpdc, 1 dc, 1 bpdc, 1 dc, 1 dc inc, 7 dc, 1 dc inc, 8 dc, 1 dc inc, 7 dc, 1 dc inc, 1 dc, 1 bpdc, 1 dc, 1 bpdc, 2 dc. (42 sts)

Row 10: 2 dc, 1 fpdc, 1 popcorn st, 1 fpdc, 3 dc, 1 dc inc, 7 dc, 1 dc inc, 8 dc, 1 dc inc, 7 dc, 1 dc inc, 3 dc, 1 fpdc, 1 popcorn st, 1 fpdc, 2 dc. (46 sts) Cut yarn.

Edging

Attach white yarn and gold yarns together, on the 1st dc of Row 10.

Row 1: Ch 1, 46 sc around the bottom, ch 1 (= corner), go up the side of the opening, working 2 sc around each dc, ch 1 (= corner), continue around the collar with 29 sc (colored marker on the 1st of these 29 sc), ch 1 (= corner), go down the side of the opening, working 2 sc around each dc, ch 1 (= corner) and fasten off with a sl st in the 1st sc. Cut yarn.

Collar

Join white and gold yarns together at the colored marker.

Row 1: Ch 1 and 1 sl st in the same st, repeat 7 times *skip 1 st, 6 dc in the same st, skip 1 st, 1 sl st*. Cut yarn, leaving a long tail of white, and weave into Row 1 of the edging (on the back side and going around 1 dc of each scallop to hold collar down).

FOR JO

FOR ANNA

Sleeves
Row 1: Attach mustard yarn to the 1st st, skip to Row 5, 9 dc, dc2tog with the 2 sts with colored marker, sl st in 3rd ch st. (10 sts)
Rows 2-5: 10 dc, sl st in 3rd ch st. (10 sts)
Switch to white and gold held together.
Row 6: Ch 1 (edge st), 10 sc, sl st in the 1st sc. (10 sts)
Row 7: Ch 1 (edge st), repeat 10 times *1 sc, 3 ch st*, sl st in the 1st sc. Cut yarn. Follow same steps to make the other sleeve.

Buttons
Sew the 4 buttons to the left front of the opening to 1 st in mustard located between the 1st and the 2nd dc (the 1st being covered by white sc from the edging) in Rows 10, 8, 6 and 4.

"BRRR" JACKET IN THREE VERSIONS:
SMALL OR LARGE COLLAR OR HOODED

INSTRUCTIONS

The number between parentheses is the number of sts at the end of the row (or rnd).

Note: Worked from the neckline down.

For All Versions

Upper Jacket
With 3.5 mm (US E-4) hook, chain 31 sts (pm in the last ch = 31st ch st).
✓ **For small collar version:** Leave a yarn tail at the beginning of the chain and attach an extra strand of yarn to the 1st dc. These 2 strands will be used later to pin down the collar.
✓ **For hooded version:** Place 1 colored marker in the 6th st of the foundation chain.
Row 1: Being sure to work into the back loop of the ch sts, 1 dc in the 5th ch from hook, 3 dc, 1 V, 2 dc, 1 V, 10 dc, 1 V, 2 dc, 1 V, 5 dc. (36 sts)
Row 2: 6 dc, 1 V, 4 dc, 1 V, 12 dc, 1 V, 4 dc, 1 V, 6 dc. (44 sts)
Row 3: 7 dc, 1 V, 6 dc, 1 V, 14 dc, 1 V, 6 dc, 1 V, 7 dc. (52 sts)
✓ In Row 3, place a colored marker under each ch st and leave them in place until working sleeves.
Row 4 (divide for arms): 8 dc, 1 dc under the ch st, skip 8 sts, 1 dc under the ch st, 16 dc, 1 dc under the ch st, skip 8 sts, 1 dc under the ch st, 8 dc. (36 sts)
Row 5: 6 dc, 1 inc, 7 dc, 1 inc, 6 dc, 1 inc, 7 dc, 1 inc, 6 dc. (40 sts)
Row 6: 7 dc, 1 inc, 7 dc, 1 inc, 8 dc, 1 inc, 7 dc, 1 inc, 7 dc. (44 sts)
Row 7: 7 dc, 1 inc, 9 dc, 1 inc, 8 dc, 1 inc, 9 dc, 1 inc, 7 dc. (48 sts)

✓ **For hooded version,** go directly to the heading for this version.

Row 8: 8 dc, 1 inc, 9 dc, 1 inc, 10 dc, 1 inc, 9 dc, 1 inc, 8 dc. (52 sts)
Cut yarn.

Small Collar Version

Sleeves
With 3.5 mm (US E-4) hook, join yarns at a colored marker, leaving a tail to sew the underarm later.
Row 1: 10 dc, sl st at the marker. (10 sts)
Note: The last dc is at the 2nd marker.
Rows 2-5: 10 dc, sl st at the marker. (10 sts)
Row 6: USING GREEN YARN (= main color) ONLY, ch 1 (edge), 10 sc, sl st in the back loop only of the 1st sc.
Row 7: Ch 1 (edge), 10 sc in back loop only, 1 sl st in the ch. Cut yarn.
Finishing the underarm: Make 2 whipstitches in the 2 dc of Row 4 with the yarn tail from beginning of sleeve.
Make another identical sleeve.

Edging around Body
With 3.5 mm (US E-4) hook, join green yarn (= main color) at the 1st dc of Row 8 on the bottom of the jacket (this is the 3rd of the 3 ch sts replacing the 1st dc), ch 1 (edge), 52 sc, ch 1 (= corner), go up the side of the opening, working 2 sc around each dc (= 16 sc), ch 1 (= corner), 28 sc around collar, ch 1 (= corner), go down other side of the opening, again working 2 sc around each dc (= 16 sc), ch 1 (= corner), 1 sl st in the 1st sc.
Cut yarn.

Collar
Fold the corner of the collar to form a pointed lapel. Thread strand of yarn on a needle. Skip 5 dc from Row 2 starting from front opening (don't forget to count the one hidden by the sc), insert needle into the head of the 5th dc and knot on wrong side to keep collar in place.
Repeat these steps with second strand.

Finishing
Sew the 4 buttons at Rows 1, 3, 5, and 7.
To button, slide buttons under the 3 edge ch sts of the corresponding rows.

Large Collar Version

Sleeves
Same as for small collar version.

Collar
With 3.5 mm (US E-4) hook, join yarns at the 1st st (unworked front loop) of the chain at the top of the jacket.
Row 1: 28 dc. (28 sts)
Row 2: Repeat 7 times *1 inc, 3 dc*. (35 sts)
Row 3: Repeat 7 times *1 inc, 4 dc*. (42 sts) USE MAHOGANY YARN (= main color) ONLY.

STITCHES AND TECHNIQUES
· Magic circle, chain stitch, slip stitch, single crochet, back loop only stitches, half double crochet, double crochet, double crochet increase or decrease: **see Stitches, page 34.**
· **1 V:** [1 dc, ch 1, and 1 dc] in the same st. Starting in Row 2, make the V under the ch st from the previous row.
· Joining with whipstitch: **see Techniques, page 39.**

Note: For versions with collar, work with 1 strand of Idéal yarn and 1 strand of Mercerized Cotton held together to give a marled appearance.
Replace the 1st dc with ch 3 and pm in the 3rd ch of each row (not indicated in pattern instructions).

Edging around Body

With the mahogany yarn from the collar, working down the front edge, ch 1 (pm), 42 sc, repeat 11 times *ch 3, 1 sl st in the base of the dc (= st between the 2 dc)*, and then 51 sc in the front loop along the bottom of the jacket, repeat 11 times *ch 3, 1 sl st in the base of the dc (= st between the 2 dc)*, 1 sl st at the marker.
Cut yarn.

Flowers

With white Coton Fifty and 2.5 mm (US B-1 or C-2) hook, begin with a magic circle.

Row 1: Repeat 5 times *ch 1, 1 hdc, ch 1, 1 sl st in the circle*.
Cut yarn and slide it in the circle.
Make 4 flowers in all.

Attach flowers to the collar, sliding the 2 yarns on either side of a st, tie 2 knots on the back side of the collar and weave in ends.

Finishing

Sew the 4 buttons at Rows 1, 3, 5, and 7.
To button, slide buttons under the 3 edge ch sts of the corresponding rows.

Hooded Version

Sleeves

With 3.5 mm (US E-4) hook, join yarns at a colored marker, leaving a tail to sew the underarm later.

Row 1: 10 dc, sl st at the marker. (10 sts) *Note: The last dc is at the 2nd marker.*

Rows 2–7: 10 dc, sl st at the marker. (10 sts)
Cut yarn. Roll up the bottom of the sleeve.

Finishing the underarm: Make 2 whipstitches in the 2 dc from Row 4 with the yarn tail from beginning of sleeve.

Make another identical sleeve.

Hood

Row 1: With 3.5 mm (US E-4) hook, join yarn at colored marker, 19 dc. (19 sts)

Note: Don't work the 6 remaining sts.

Row 2: 2 dc, 1 inc, 4 dc, 1 inc, 3 dc, 1 inc, 4 dc, 1 inc, 2 dc. (23 sts)

Row 3: 3 dc, 1 inc, 4 dc, 1 inc, 5 dc, 1 inc, 4 dc, 1 inc, 3 dc. (27 sts)

Row 4: 4 dc, 1 inc, repeat 3 times *5 dc, 1 inc*, 4 dc. (31 sts)

Rows 5–7: 31 dc. (31 sts)

Row 8: 3 dc, repeat 9 times *dc2tog, 1 dc*, 1 dc. (22 sts)

Row 9: 3 dc, repeat 6 times *1 dc2tog, 1 dc*, 1 dc. (16 sts)

Row 10: 1 inc, 1 dc, dc2tog, 1 dc, repeat 2 times *dc3tog*, 1 dc, dc2tog, 1 dc, 1 inc. (12 sts)
Cut a strand of yarn for sewing.

Thread needle and sew together with whipstitch, inserting needle first in the last st and then in the 1st st of Row 10. Continue in same manner for 4 more sts. Tie knot on back.

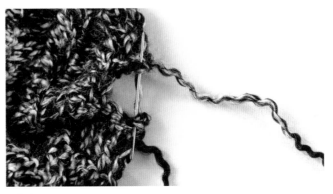

Edging

With 3.5 mm (US E-4) hook, attach Idéal yarn at 1st dc of Row 7 on the bottom of the jacket (this is the 3rd of the 3 ch sts replacing the 1st dc), ch 1 (edge), 48 sc, ch 1 (= corner), go up the left side of the opening, repeating 3 times *[1 sc, ch 1 (= buttonhole) and 1 sc] around 1 dc, 2 sc around the following dc*, [1 sc, ch 1 (= buttonhole) and 1 sc] around the last dc, ch 1 (= corner), 4 sc around the collar in the sts from the starting chain, sc 2 together (in 1 ch st and the following ch st, which has already been worked; it corresponds to the colored marker for the hood). Continue around the hood, working 2 sc around each dc (= 40 sc), sc2tog as above, 3 sc in the ch sts, ch 1 (= corner), and then go down other side of the opening, again working 2 sc around each dc (= 14 sc), ch 1 (= corner), 1 sl st in the 1st sc.
Cut yarn.

Finishing

On the left front of opening, sew the 4 buttons to the 2 sc of the border at Rows 1, 3, 5, and 7.
To button, slide buttons under the ch st between the 2 edging sc of the corresponding rows.

CAPE

INSTRUCTIONS

The number between parentheses is the number of sts at the end of the row.

With yarn **a** and 4 mm (US G-6) hook, chain 53 sts (pm in the last ch st).

Row 1: 1 dc in the 5th ch, 48 dc. (50 sts)

Row 2: Ch 1 to turn, repeat 25 times *1 sc, 1 sc inc*. (75 sts)

Row 3: 1 dc inc, repeat 14 times *ch 2, skip 2 sts, 1 dc inc, 1 dc, 1 dc inc*, ch 2, skip 2 sts, 1 dc, 1 dc inc (= 105 sts), remove hook and PM in the loop (keep yarn **a** on hold).

Row 4: With 5 mm (US H-8) hook, attach yarn **b** to the 1st skipped stitch in Row 3 (at start of row), repeat 14 times *2 dc in the ch sts in previous row, ch 2*, 2 dc in the next ch space (= 58 sts), remove hook and pm in the loop (keep yarn **b** on hold).

Row 5: Reinsert 4 mm (US G-6) hook in the mustard loop with marker in Row 3. With yarn **a**, work 2 dc in the dc from Row 3, repeat 14 times *ch 2, skip the dc in yarn **b** from the previous row, work dc into the dc in yarn **a** from Row 3 AND working over and encircling the 2 ch sts in yarn **b** from the last row*, ch 2, skip 2 sts, 3 dc in the dc from row 3 (= 105 sts), remove hook and pm in the loop (keep yarn **a** on hold).

Row 6: Reinsert 5 mm (US H-8) hook in white loop with marker. In yarn **b**, repeat 14 times *2 dc in the 2 dc in yarn **b** AND encircling the 2 ch sts in yarn **a**, ch 2, skip the 5 dc in yarn **a** from the last row*, 2 dc in the dc from Row 4 (= 58 sts), remove hook and pm in the loop (keep yarn **b** on hold).

Key

◄   Cut yarn.

○   **1 chain stitch:** Yarn over, draw yarn through loop on the hook.

×   **1 single crochet:** Insert hook in st, yo and pull through the st, yo and pull yarn through all loops on the hook.

⊤   **1 double crochet:** Yarn over, then insert hook in st, yo and pull through st, and then repeat *yo, pull through 2 loops*.

⋙   **1 single crochet increase:** Work 2 sc into the same st.

▨   Mustard yarn and 4 mm (US G-6) hook

▬   White yarn and 5 mm (US H-8) hook

SUPPLIES

• Bergère de France Idéal yarn (#3 light weight; 30% acrylic, 30% polyamide, 40% combed wool; 136 yd/124 m per 1.8 oz/50 g) in Girolle (mustard) (**a**)

• Bergère de France Plume yarn (#5 bulky weight; 11% combed wool, 42% acrylic, 47% polyamide; 87 yd/79.5 m per 1.8 oz/50 g) in Tulle (white) (**b**)

• Bergère de France Ciboulette yarn (#1 super fine weight; 75% acrylic, 25% wool; 252 yd/230 m per 1.8 oz/50 g) in Diamant (white) (**c**)

• 2.5 mm (US B-1 or C-2), 4 mm (US G-6), and 5 mm (US H-8) hooks

Note: Ciboulette yarn can be replaced by Idéal in Everest (white).

STITCHES AND TECHNIQUES

• Chain stitch, double crochet, double crochet, or single crochet increase: **see Stitches, page 34.**

• **Circle tab:** Ch 3, repeat 5 times *yo, insert hook into the 1st ch st, yo and pull through 2 loops*, and 1 sl st also in the 1st ch st.

Note: Starting in Row 3, replace the 1st dc with ch 3 and pm in the 3rd ch (not indicated in pattern instructions).

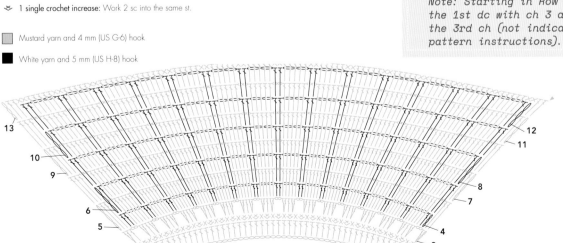

TIP

Instead of making a tie, you could use a cord, a bias tape, etc. Weave the tie through the top of the cape, place the cape on the doll, and then pull on the cord to adjust and even out the gathers.

Row 7: Reinsert 4 mm (US G-6) hook in the mustard loop with marker. With yarn **a**, work 3 dc in the dc from the next to the last row, repeat 14 times *ch 2, skip the dc in yarn **b** from the previous Row, work dc into the dc in yarn **a** from Row 5 AND working over and encircling the 2 ch sts in yarn **b** from the last row*, ch 2, skip 2 sts, 2 dc in the dc from the next to the last row (= 105 sts), remove hook and pm in the loop (keep yarn **a** on hold).

Rows 8–12: Continue in this same pattern, and at the end of Row 12 (see diagram), cut yarn **b**.

Row 13: Reinsert 4 mm (US G-6) hook in the mustard loop with marker. With yarn **a**, work 3 dc in the dc from 2 rows below, repeat 14 times *2 sc in the dc in yarn **b**, 5 dc in the 5 sts in yarn **a** AND encircling the 2 ch sts in yarn **b***, 2 sc in the dc in yarn **b**, 2 dc (= 105 sts).
Cut yarn.

Tie

With yarn **c** and 2.5 mm (US B-1 or C-2) hook, make 1 circle tab, crochet a 25 in/65 cm long chain and make another circle tab. Cut yarn.

SUPPLIES

FOR JOSETTE

· Bergère de France Ciboulette yarn (#1 super fine weight; 75% acrylic, 25% wool; 252 yd/230 m per 1.8 oz/50 g) in Diamant (white)
· Bergère de France Coton Fifty yarn (#2 fine weight; 4 ply; 50% cotton, 50% acrylic; 153 yd/140 m per 1.8 oz/50 g) in Cytise (yellow)
· Small beads (like seed beads)
· 2.5 mm (US B-1 or C-2) hook
· Extra fine needle

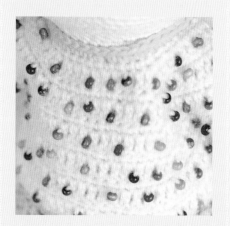

—

SHORT-SLEEVED TOPS

—

MULTICOLOR BEAD T-SHIRT

To easily thread Ciboulette yarn onto the needle

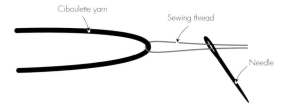

Ciboulette yarn

Sewing thread

Needle

INSTRUCTIONS

The number between parentheses is the number of sts at the end of the row (or rnd).

Body

Slide forty or so beads onto the ball of white (Ciboulette) yarn. Begin by chaining 41 sts.

Row 1 (work in the back loop of the chain): 1 sc in the 2nd ch st, 39 sc. (40 sts)

Row 2: Repeat 5 times *7 dc, 1 sc inc*. (45 sts)

Row 3: Ch 1, repeat 5 times *8 sc, 1 sc inc*. (50 sts)

Row 4: Repeat 5 times *9 dc, 1 sc inc*. (55 sts)

Row 5: Ch 1, repeat 5 times *10 sc, 1 sc inc. (60 sts)

Row 6: Repeat 5 times *11 dc, 1 dc inc*. (65 sts)

Row 7: Ch 1, repeat 5 times *12 sc, 1 sc inc*. (70 sts)

Row 8: Repeat 5 times *13 dc, 1 dc inc*. (75 sts)

Rnd 9: Ch 1, 12 sc, skip 12 sts (= arm, colored marker in the 1st skipped st), 27 sc, skip 12 sts (= arm, colored marker in the last skipped st), 12 sc, close with sl st at the marker. (51 sts)

Rnd 10: TURN WORK, 6 dc, repeat 3 times *1 dc inc, 12 dc*, 1 dc inc, 5 dc, sl st at the marker. (55 sts)

Rnd 11: Ch 1, TURN WORK, 55 sc, sl st at the marker. (55 sts)

Rnd 12: TURN WORK, repeat 5 times *10 dc, 1 dc inc*, sl st at the marker. (60 sts) Switch to yellow at the sl st.

Rnd 13: Ch 1, TURN WORK, 60 sc, 1 sl st at the marker (= 60 sts), fasten off with ch 1 and cut yarn.

Sleeve Edging

Left Arm

Join yellow yarn at marker, ch 1, 12 sc, 2 sc at the underarm, 1 sl st in the 1st sc. (14 sts) Cut yarn.

Right Arm

Join yellow yarn at marker, ch 1, 1 sc, 2 sc at the underarm, 12 sc, 1 sl st in the 1st sc. (14 sts) Cut yarn.

Collar

Join yellow yarn at 1st st (by tail at beginning of chain), ch 1, 9 sc, repeat 2 times *8 sc, dc2tog*, 9 sc. Cut yarn.

TRICOLOR TOP

INSTRUCTIONS

Note: Worked from the neckline down.

Back

With 4 mm (US G-6) hook and the 1st color, chain 25 sts (pm in the last ch st), and then finish the rest of the top with the 3.5 mm (US E-4) hook.

Row 1: [1 dc in the 4th ch st and 1 dc] in the same st, repeat 6 times *ch 1, skip 2 sts, 3 dc in the next st*, ch 1, skip 2 sts, 2 dc in the last st.

STITCHES AND TECHNIQUES

· Chain stitch, slip stitch, single crochet, double crochet, single crochet or double crochet increase, single crochet 2 together: **see Stitches, page 34.**

· Place beads randomly, only on dc rows, and for a less aligned look, alternate *slide 1 bead after 1 dc* and *slide 1 bead before the last yo of the dc*. The beads are placed at the back of the work.

Tip: To easily thread the Ciboulette yarn onto the needle, fold the white yarn in half, loop sewing thread around the folded end, and then thread the 2 ends of the sewing thread into the needle and pull (see drawing on page 76).

· Changing colors: **see Techniques, page 39.**

Notes: On even rows (WS), replace the 1st dc with ch 3 and pm in the 3rd ch.

On odd rows (RS), the ch st at the beginning of the row does not replace the sc (edge); place a marker on the 1st sc.

SUPPLIES

· **Version A:** Bergère de France Idéal yarn (#3 light weight; 30% acrylic, 30% polyamide, 40% combed wool; 136 yd/124 m per 1.8 oz/50 g) in the following colors: Vannerie (beige), Beige rose (dusty rose), and Sequoia (mahogany)

· **Version B:** Bergère de France Coton Fifty yarn (#2 fine weight; 4 ply; 50% cotton, 50% acrylic; 153 yd/140 m per 1.8 oz/50 g) in the following colors: Coco (white), Berlingot (pink), and Bengale (fuchsia)

· 2 small buttons (for each version)

· 3.5 mm (US E-4) and 4 mm (US G-6) (only for foundation chain) hooks

CLOTHING & ACCESSORIES

STITCHES AND TECHNIQUES

· Chain stitch, single crochet, double crochet: **see Stitches, page 34.**
· Changing colors: **see Techniques, page 39.**
· Color patterns:
Version A: Repeat *1 row dusty rose, 2 rows beige, 1 row mahogany*
Version B: 1 row fuchsia, 2 rows pink, 1 row white, 1 row fuchsia, 1 row white, 1 row pink, 1 row fuchsia

TIP

For larger buttons, make 2 ch sts for the buttonhole instead of one.

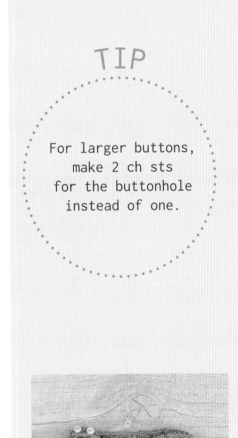

Row 2: Ch 4, (pm in the 3rd ch st), repeat 7 times *3 dc in the ch-1 space, ch 1*, 1 dc at the marker.
Row 3: Ch 3, 1 dc in the ch space, ch 1, repeat 6 times *3 dc in the ch-1 space, ch 1*, 1 dc in the last ch space, 1 dc at the marker.
Rows 4–8: Repeat Rows 2 and 3.

Front
Same as the **back**.

Sides
Place the **back** on the **front**, and crocheting into the 2 pieces at the same time, join the dusty rose (or fuchsia) yarn to the edge of the last sts of Row 8: ch 1, work 2 sc around the back and front st of Rows 8 through 4 (so don't close up the entire side). Cut yarn. Follow same steps on the other side.

Right Shoulder
Inserting hook through 2 pieces at same time, join the dusty rose (or fuchsia) yarn between the last 2 dc of **Row 1**: ch 1 (edge), 1 sc, 2 sc in the ch space (2 ch sts not worked), 1 sc in the middle st of the 3 dc, 2 sc in the ch space. Cut yarn.

Left Shoulder

Back with Buttonholes
After right shoulder, skip 3 ch spaces, AND crocheting only on the **back**, join matching yarn in the 4th ch space: ch 1, repeat 2 times *2 sc in the ch space, ch 1 loosely (= buttonhole)*, 1 sc in the last st. Cut yarn.

Front with Buttons
On **front** side, sew the buttons to the 2nd dc and to the center st of the 3 dc.

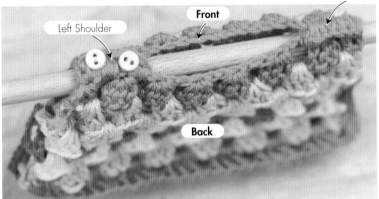

Right Shoulder
Front
Left Shoulder
Back

LACE TOP

INSTRUCTIONS

Bottom of the Body

Begin by chaining 72 sts and join in the round with a sl st in the 1st ch st.

Rnd 1: [Ch 4 (= 1 dc and 1 ch-1 space, pm in ch space) and 1 dc] in the same st, repeat 8 times *skip 3 sts, 1 VA, skip 3 sts, 1 VB*, skip 3 sts, 1 VA, sl st at the marker.

Rnd 2: [Ch 4 (= 1 dc and 1 ch-1 space, pm in ch space) and 1 dc] in the same ch space, repeat 8 times *3 tr in the ch-3 space, 1 VB in the ch-1 space, sl st at the marker.

Rnd 3: [Ch 4 (= 1 dc and 1 ch-1 space, pm in ch space) and 1 dc] in the same ch space, repeat 8 times *1 VA between the 2 tr at middle of the shell, 1 VB in the ch-1 sp*, 1 VA between the 2 tr at the middle of the next shell, sl st at the marker.

Rnds 4-6: Repeat Rnds 2 and 3, ending with Rnd 2. Then divide the work in half.

Front

Row 7: [Ch 4 (= 1 dc and 1 ch-1 space) and 1 dc] in the same ch space, repeat 4 times *1 VA between the 2 tr at middle of the shell, 1 VB in ch-1 sp*, DO NOT WORK REMAINING STS.

Row 8: Ch 1 to turn, [1 sl st, ch 4 (= 1 dc and 1 ch-1 space) and 1 dc] in the same ch space, repeat 4 times *6 tr in the ch-3 space, 1 VB in the ch-1 space*.

Place colored marker between the 2 tr at middle of the 1st and last shells (for collar).

First Shoulder

Row 9: Ch 1 to turn, [1 sl st, ch 4 (= 1 dc and 1 ch-1 space) and 1 dc] in the same ch space, 1 VA between the 2 tr at the middle of the shell from the previous row.

Row 10: Ch 1 to turn, 1 sl st in the ch-3 space, ch 4 (= 1st tr), 5 tr in the ch space, 1 dc, ch 1, 1 dc in the ch-1 space. Cut yarn, leaving a long tail for sewing the shoulder.

Second Shoulder

Join yarn at the last ch space in Row 8, and then repeat Rows 9 and 10.

Back

Join yarn between 2 tr at middle of the 1st shell of Rnd 6.

Row 7: [Ch 6 (= 1 dc and 1 ch-3 space) and 1 dc] in the same ch space, repeat *1 VB in the ch-1 sp, 1 VA between the 2 tr at middle of the shell*.

SUPPLIES

- Mercerized cotton (100% Egyptian cotton; 617 yd/565 m per 3.5 oz/100 g) in white
- Thin white elastic thread
- 2 mm hooks

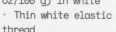

STITCHES AND TECHNIQUES

- Chain stitch, slip stitch, double crochet, triple crochet: **see Stitches, page 34.**
- **1 VA:** [1 dc, ch 3, and 1 dc] in the same st.
- **1 VB:** [1 dc, ch 1, and 1 dc] in the same st.
- Joining with whipstitch: **see Techniques, page 39.**

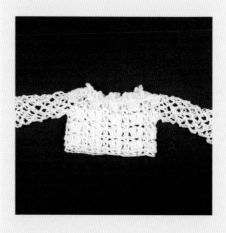

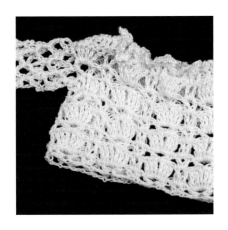

Row 8: Ch 1 to turn, [1 sl st, ch 4 (= 1st tr) and 5 tr] in the same ch space, repeat 4 times *1 dc, ch 1, 1 dc in the ch-1 space, 6 tr in the ch-3 space*.

Place 1 colored marker in the ch-1 space of the 1st and last VB (for the collar).

Cut yarn, leaving a long tail for sewing the shoulder.

Sew the **front** 9 shoulder sts to those on the back using the whipstitch.

Collar

Join yarn at one of the markers from Row 8.

Rnd 1: Ch 3 (pm in the 3rd ch st), 1 dc in each st and in the marked ch-1 spaces, and work 5 dc in the sides of the dc at the shoulders (2 times on each side), 1 sl st at the marker.

Rnd 2: Ch 1, work *1 sc and 3 ch sts* in each st, 1 sl st in the 1st sc.

Fasten off with ch 1 and cut yarn.

Thread the elastic on the needle and pass it between 2 dc from Rnd 1 of the collar on the back side, and then slide through, alternating 1 time over 1 dc and 1 time under, all the way around. Put the top on the doll. Pull on elastic to tighten the neckline, and then make 2 knots to secure. Weave in ends of elastic on wrong side.

Sleeves

Join yarn to side of 1 dc at the armhole.

Rnd 1: Ch 1 (edge), 1 sc (pm), ch 5, repeat 5 times *1 sc around the next dc, ch 5*, 1 sc around the next dc, close the rnd with 2 ch sts and 1 dc at the marker. (7 ch spaces)

Rnds 2–12: Ch 1, 1 sc (pm), ch 5, repeat 5 times *1 sc in the ch space, ch 5*, 1 sc in the ch space, close the rnd with 2 ch sts and 1 dc at the marker. (7 ch spaces)

Cut yarn.

Make another identical sleeve.

CROP TOP

INSTRUCTIONS

The number between parentheses is the number of sts at the end of the rnd (or row).

Bottom of Body

In orange, chain 54 sts and join in the round with a sl st in the 1st ch st.

Rnd 1: Ch 1, repeat 9 times *1 sc, skip 2 sts, 5 dc in the same st, skip 2 sts*, sl st at the marker, switching to black at the sl st. (54 sts) KEEP ORANGE YARN ON HOLD.

Rnd 2: Repeat 9 times *5 dc in the sc, skip 2 sts, 1 sc, skip 2 sts*, 1 sl st at the marker, switching to orange at the sl st. (54 sts) KEEP BLACK YARN ON HOLD.

SUPPLIES

- Bergère de France Coton Fifty yarn (#2 fine weight; 4 ply; 50% cotton, 50% acrylic; 153 yd/140 m per 1.8 oz/50 g) in Zan (black) and Gingembre (orange)
- 1 small snap
- 3 mm (US C-2 or D-3) hook

FOR EMORY

Rnd 3: Sl st to the 3rd dc of the previous rnd, ch 1, repeat 9 times *1 sc, skip 2 sts, 5 dc in the sc, skip 2 sts*, sl st at the marker, switching to black at the sl st. (54 sts) KEEP ORANGE YARN ON HOLD.

Rnd 4: Repeat Rnd 2, picking up the black yarn.

Rnd 5: Repeat Rnd 3, picking up the orange yarn, and during this rnd, place a colored marker on the 43rd st. Cut orange yarn, keep black yarn.

First Half-Back (Armholes and Back Opening)

Row 6: With black yarn, 2 dc on the sc, skip 2 sts, 1 sc, skip 2 sts, 5 dc in the same st, skip 2 sts, 1 sc, skip 2 sts, 2 dc on the sc (switch to orange on the last dc). KEEP BLACK YARN ON HOLD.

Row 7: Ch 1, 1 sc, skip 1 st, 5 dc in the same st, skip 2 sts, 1 sc, skip 2 sts, 5 dc in the same st, skip 1 st, 1 sc (switch to black on the last sc). KEEP ORANGE YARN ON HOLD.

Row 8: Repeat Row 6.

Row 9: Repeat Row 7.

Cut yarns.

Second Half-Back

Join black yarn at the colored marker and repeat Rows 6-9.

Front (Armholes)

Join black yarn at the 1st dc of the 1st **half-back**.

Row 6: 2 dc, skip 2 sts, 1 sc, skip 2 sts, 5 dc in the same st, skip 2 sts, 1 sc, skip 2 sts, 2 dc (switch to orange at the last dc). KEEP BLACK YARN ON HOLD.

Row 7: Ch 1, 1 sc, skip 1 st, 5 dc in the same st, skip 2 sts, repeat 3 times *1 sc, skip 2 sts, 5 dc in the same st, skip 2 sts*, 1 sc, skip 2 sts, 5 dc in the same st, skip 1 st, 1 sc, (switch to black at the last sc). KEEP ORANGE YARN ON HOLD.

Row 8: Repeat Row 6.

Row 9: Repeat Row 7.

Cut yarn.

Seaming Shoulders

First Shoulder

With black, join at the last st in the **front**, ch 3 (= 1st dc), repeat 6 times *remove hook from the loop, insert hook in the corresponding st on the **back**, 1 sl st, 1 dc on the **front*** (= 7 sts). Cut yarn.

Second Shoulder

Repeat from other side, reversing it, i.e.:
With black, join at the last st in the **back**, ch 3 (= 1st dc), repeat 6 times *remove hook from the loop, insert hook in the corresponding st on the **front**, 1 sl st, 1 dc on the **back*** (= 7 sts). Cut yarn.

Sew the snap to the 1st and last dc of the **back** opening.

STITCHES AND TECHNIQUES

· Chain stitch, slip stitch, single crochet, double crochet: see **Stitches, page 34.**

· Changing colors: see **Techniques, page 39.**

Notes: The ch st at the beginning of the rnd/row is an edge st. Replace the 1st dc with ch 3 (not indicated in the instructions). Pm on the 3rd ch st of each even rnd or row, or on the 1st sc of each odd rnd or row (not indicated in the instructions).

· **Stripes:** Alternate 1 row in orange and 1 row in black.

SUPPLIES

- **Version A:** Bergère de France Coton Fifty yarn (#2 fine weight; 4 ply; 50% cotton, 50% acrylic; 153 yd/140 m per 1.8 oz/50 g) in the following colors: Perle (gray) and Berlingot (pink), or Coco (white) and Gingembre (orange); Bergère de France Metalika yarn (38% polyamide, 62% metal-effect polyester; 710 yd/649 m per 0.9 oz/25.5 g) in Libellule (iridescent) (optional)
- **Version B:** Bergère de France Pure Douceur yarn (#4 medium weight; 5% wool, 37% polyamide, 58% superkid mohair; 273 yd/250 m per 1.8 oz/50 g) in Peau (nude)
- 1 small snap (for each version)
- 3.5 mm (US E-4) and 4 mm (US G-6) hooks

STITCHES AND TECHNIQUES

- Chain stitch, slip stitch, single crochet, single crochet 2 together, double crochet: **see Stitches, page 34.**
- Changing colors, working in a spiral, joining with whipstitch: **see Techniques, page 39.**

Notes: For version A, work holding the Metalika yarn together with the gray or white yarn.
The 1st ch st is a turning ch and does not replace the 1st sc.
For Rnd 1 through Rnd 13, pm on the 1st sc of each rnd (just after the ch st). At the end of the rnd, when working the sl st, there should be 2 sts: the sl st and the ch st from the beginning of the previous rnd.
For Rows 14 through 18, pm in the ch st at the beginning of the row. Also, join the yarn in the ch st, ch 1 (pm), and then work in the following sc.

FOR VIOLET

FOR NINA

SWEATERS

RUFFLED COLLAR SWEATER

INSTRUCTIONS

Note: This sweater is worked bottom up.

The number between parentheses is the number of sts at the end of the rnd (or row).

Body

With pink (or white, or nude) and with 4 mm (US G-6) hook, chain 56 sts and join in the round with a sl st in the 1st ch st.

Rnd 1: Ch 3 (= 1st dc, pm on the 3rd ch st), 55 dc, sl st at the marker, switching to gray (or orange). (56 sts)

Rnds 2-3: Ch 1, 56 sc, sl st at the marker. (56 sts)

Note: Starting in Rnd 3, pm on the 1st sc of each rnd and work in the back loops only, up to and including Rnd 18.

Rnd 4: Ch 1, repeat 4 times *12 sc, sc2tog*, sl st at the marker. (52 sts)

Rnd 5: Ch 1, 52 sc, sl st at the marker. (52 sts)

Rnd 6: Ch 1, repeat 4 times *11 sc, sc2tog*, sl st at the marker. (48 sts)

Rnd 7: Ch 1, 48 sc, sl st at the marker. (48 sts)

Rnd 8: Ch 1, repeat 4 times *10 sc, sc2tog*, sl st at the marker. (44 sts)

Rnd 9: Ch 1, 44 sc, sl st at the marker. (44 sts)

Rnd 10: Ch 1, repeat 4 times *9 sc, sc2tog*. (40 sts)

Rnd 11: Ch 1, 40 sc, sl st at the marker. (40 sts)

Rnd 12: Ch 1, 9 sc, sc2tog, 18 sc, sc2tog, 9 sc. (38 sts)

Rnd 13: Ch 1, 38 sc, sl st at the marker. (38 sts)

Row 14: Ch 1, 9 sc, ch 11 (= armhole) skip 1 st, 18 sc, ch 11 (= armhole), skip 1 st, 9 sc. (58 sts) Cut yarn.

Row 15: Join yarn at marker, ch 1, 9 sc, 11 sc on the 11 ch sts, 18 sc, 11 sc on the 11 ch sts, 9 sc. (58 sts) Cut yarn.

Row 16: Join yarn at marker, ch 1, 4 sc, repeat 2 times *sc2tog, 8 sc*, sc2tog, 7 sc, repeat 2 times *sc2tog, 8 sc*, sc2tog, 3 sc. (52 sts) Cut yarn.

Row 17: Join yarn at marker, ch 1, 3 sc, sc2tog, 6 sc, sc2tog, 7 sc, sc2tog, 8 sc, sc2tog, 7 sc, sc2tog, 6 sc, sc2tog, 3 sc. (46 sts) Cut yarn.

Row 18: Join yarn at marker, ch 1, 3 sc, repeat 2 times *sc2tog, 6 sc*, sc2tog, 5 sc, repeat 2 times *sc2tog, 6 sc*, sc2tog, 2 sc. (40 sts) DO NOT CUT YARN.

Row 19: Ch 1 to turn, repeat 8 times *3 sc, sc2tog*. (32 sts) Place colored marker at the 1st and last sts of the row (= placement of snap). DO NOT CUT YARN.

Collar

Continue with 3.5 mm (US E-4) hook.

Row 19 (in the free front loops of the Row 18 sts): Ch 1, repeat 16 times *1 sc, 2 sc in the same st* (OR, for more ruffles: work 2 sc in each st). (48 sts / 64 sts)

Row 20: Ch 3, turn, 1 dc in the same st, repeat 48 (64) times *2 dc in the same st*. (96 sts / 128 sts)

Row 21: Ch 3 (= 1st dc), turn, 95 (127) dc. (96 sts / 128 sts) Switch to pink (or white) at the last dc.

Row 22: Ch 1 to turn, 96 (128) sc. (96 sts / 128 sts) Cut yarn.

Sleeves

With pink (or white) and 4 mm (US G-6) hook, ch 15 sts and join in the round with a sl st in the 1st ch st.

Rnd 1: Ch 3 (= 1st dc), 14 dc, 1 sl st in the 3rd ch st, switching to gray (or orange). (15 sts)

Rnd 2: Ch 1, 15 sc in back loops only of the sts from the previous rnd. (15 sts)

Rnds 3-16 (working in spiral): 15 sc in back loops only of the sts from the previous rnd. (15 sts) Cut yarn, leaving a long tail for sewing. Make another identical sleeve.

FINISHING

Sew on the two sides of the snap at the colored markers. Seam the sleeves with whipstitch, working into the back loop of the stitches.

BOBBLE PULLOVER

INSTRUCTIONS

The number between parentheses is the number of sts at the end of the row.

Front

Chain 24 sts, leaving a long tail of yarn for sewing.

Row 1: 1 sc in the 2nd ch st (pm), 22 sc. (23 sts)

Row 2: Ch 1, repeat 5 times *3 sc, 1 bobble*, 3 sc. (23 sts)

Row 3: Ch 1, 23 sc. (23 sts)

Row 4: Ch 1, 1 sc, repeat 5 times *1 bobble, 3 sc*, 1 bobble, 1 sc. (23 sts)

Row 5: Ch 1, 23 sc. (23 sts)

Rows 6-13: Repeat Rows 2-5.

Row 14: Ch 1, sc2tog, 1 sc, repeat 4 times *1 bobble, 3 sc*, 1 bobble, 1 sc, sc2tog. (21 sts)

✓ Place a colored marker on the 2 sc2tog for sewing side seams.

Row 15: Ch 1, sc2tog, 17 sc, sc2tog. (19 sts)

Row 16: Ch 1, sc2tog, 1 sc, repeat 3 times *1 bobble, 3 sc*, 1 bobble, 1 sc, sc2tog. (17 sts)

Row 17: Ch 1, 17 sc. (17 sts)

SUPPLIES

· Bergère de France Idéal yarn (#3 light weight; 30% acrylic, 30% polyamide, 40% combed wool; 136 yd/124 m per 1.8 oz/50 g) in Citronnier (lime green) or Persan (blue)

· 2 small snaps
· 4 mm (US G-6) hook

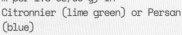

FOR FAWNTINE

STITCHES AND TECHNIQUES

- Chain stitch, slip stitch, single crochet, single crochet bobble, single crochet 2 together: **see Stitches, page 34.**
- Joining with whipstitch: **see Techniques, page 39.**

Notes: Odd rows are on the right side of the work and even rows on the wrong side of the work.

The ch st at the beginning of the row is an edge st used only to turn the work.

Pm on the 1st sc of the row (not indicated in the instructions).

TIP

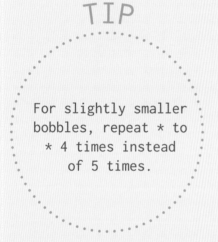

For slightly smaller bobbles, repeat * to * 4 times instead of 5 times.

Row 18: Ch 1, 4 sc, repeat 2 times *1 bobble, 3 sc*, 1 bobble, 4 sc. (17 sts)
Row 19: Ch 1, 17 sc. (17 sts)
✓ Place colored marker on the 4th sc.
Row 20: Ch 1, 1 sl st (place colored marker), 1 sc, 1 bobble, 1 sc. (4 sts) DON'T WORK REMAINING STS.
Row 21: Ch 1, 3 sc. (3 sts) DON'T WORK THE SL ST.
Row 22: Ch 1, 3 sc (= **left shoulder**). Cut yarn.
Join yarn on back side of the work at the marker from Row 19, and then:
Row 20-b: Ch 1, 1 sc, 1 bobble, 1 sc. (4 sts) DON'T WORK THE LAST ST and place colored marker on top.
Row 21-b and 22-b: Ch 1, 3 sc (= **right shoulder**). Cut yarn.

Back
Work as for the **Front** up to and including Row 17.
Row 18: Ch 1, 1 sl st (place colored marker), 3 sc. (3 sts)
Rows 19-20: Ch 1, 3 sc (= **shoulder**). Cut yarn.
Join yarn at the 2nd sc of Row 17 and place colored marker on the 1st sc of Row 17.
Rows 18-20-b: Ch 1, 3 sc (= **shoulder**). Cut yarn.

Seaming the Body
Seam the sides of the body with whipstitch, starting from the bottom up to the colored markers.
Join the last unworked st (markers) of the **back** to the corresponding st on the **front** (= shoulder side outside st): insert needle in the 2 sts of the 2 colored markers at the same time, and then tie 2 knots on the back side.
Sew the snaps to the last row of the shoulders.

Sleeves
Begin by chaining 16 sts.
Row 1: 1 sc in the 2nd ch st (pm), 14 sc. (15 sts)
Row 2: Ch 1, repeat 3 times *3 sc, 1 bobble*, 3 sc. (15 sts)
Row 3: Ch 1, 15 sc. (15 sts)
Row 4: Ch 1, 1 sc, repeat 3 times *1 bobble, 3 sc*, 1 bobble, 1 sc. (15 sts)
Row 5: Ch 1, 15 sc. (15 sts)
Rows 6-19: Repeat Rows 2-5.
Cut yarn, leaving a long tail for sewing.
Make another identical sleeve.

Seaming the Sleeves
Fold each sleeve in half lengthwise, place marker at the center stitch then position the sleeve so the center st marker is at the top of the shoulder (hold stitches together with a marker). Use long tail of yarn to seam with whipstitch starting at the underarm. Then continue along the entire length of the sleeve.

SAILOR SWEATER

INSTRUCTIONS

Note: This sweater is worked bottom up, in stripes.

The number between parentheses is the number of sts at the end of the rnd (or row).

Bottom of Body
Begin by chaining 46 sts and join in the round with a sl st.
Rnds 1-13: Ch 1, 46 sc, sl st at the marker. (46 sts)
Rnd 14: Ch 1, 1 invisible dec, 19 sc, 2 invisible dec, 19 sc, 1 invisible dec, sl st at the marker. (42 sts)
Then separate to work the back and then the front in rows.

Back
Row 15: Ch 1, 1 invisible dec, 17 sc, 1 invisible dec. (19 sts) DON'T WORK THE REMAINING STS.
Row 16: Ch 1 to turn, 1 invisible dec, 15 sc, 1 invisible dec. (17 sts)
Rows 17-19: Ch 1 to turn, 17 sc. (17 sts)
Row 20: Ch 1 to turn, 3 sc (pm), (= 3 sts, **first shoulder**), 1 sc (pm for seaming), 3 sc. DON'T WORK REMAINING STS.
Row 21: Ch 1 to turn, 3 sc, don't work the st with marker. (3 sts)
Row 22: Ch 1 to turn, 3 sc. (3 sts) Cut yarns.
Skip 9 sts of Row 20 and join yarn at 4th sc from the end and repeat Rows 20-22.
Second shoulder: Join yarn at 1st st of Row 19 and repeat Rows 20-22.

Front
Row 15: Join yarn at Row 14, ch 1, 1 invisible dec, 17 sc, 1 invisible dec. (19 sts)
Row 16: Ch 1 to turn, 1 invisible dec, 15 sc, 1 invisible dec. (17 sts)
Row 17: Ch 1 to turn, 17 sc. (17 sts)
Row 18: Ch 1 to turn, 5 sc, 1 invisible dec. (6 sts) DON'T WORK THE REMAINING STS.
Row 19: Ch 1 to turn, 1 invisible dec, 4 sc. (5 sts)
Row 20: Ch 1 to turn, 1 sc (= marker), 2 sc, 1 invisible dec. (4 sts)
Row 21: Ch 1 to turn, 3 sc. (3 sts)
Row 22: Ch 1 to turn, 3 sc. (3 sts)
The **first shoulder** is finished. Cut yarns.
Second shoulder: Join yarn at 1st st of Row 17 and repeat Rows 18-22.
Using whipstitch, join the last unworked st (markers) of the **back** and the **front** (= shoulder side outside st) on each side.

SUPPLIES

• Bergère de France Idéal yarn (#3 light weight; 30% acrylic, 30% polyamide, 40% combed wool; 136 yd/124 m per 1.8 oz/50 g) in Cendre (gray) and Persan (blue)
• 4 mm (US G-6) hook

FOR AVERY

STITCHES AND TECHNIQUES
• Chain stitch, slip stitch, single crochet, invisible decrease: **see Stitches, page 34.**
• Changing colors, joining with whipstitch: **see Techniques, page 39.**
• **Stripes:** Odd rnds/rows in gray, even rnds/rows in blue; then starting in Row 15, hide the yarn as you go.

Notes: The ch st at the beginning of the row is an edge st that is not to be worked later.

Always place a marker in the 1st sc or dec of the rnd/row.

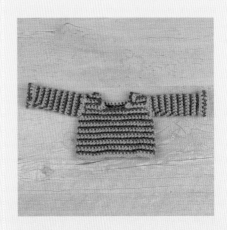

Sleeves

Chain 15 sts, join to work in the round with a sl st in the 1st ch.

Rnds 1-21: Ch 1 (edge), 15 sc. (15 sts)

Cut yarn, leaving a long tail for sewing.

Make another identical sleeve.

Use whipstitch to sew to armholes. Sew snaps to shoulders.

GRANITE STITCH PULLOVER IN THREE VERSIONS:

STRIPED, EMBROIDERED, WITH PETER PAN COLLAR AND PUFFED SLEEVES

INSTRUCTIONS

Note: This sweater is worked top down.

The number between parentheses is the number of sts at the end of the row (or rnd).

Basic Body for All Versions

With mahogany (lime green, blue, or brown), chain 29 sts.

Row 1: 1 sc (pm) in 2nd ch from hook, 27 sc (= 28 sts), and then make **buttonhole**: ch 3, turn, sl st in the last sc.

Row 2: Ch 2 (pm in ch space), skip 1 st, 1 sc, ch 1, skip 1 st, 1 inc, ch 1, skip 1 st, 1 sc, ch 1, skip 1 st, 1 inc, repeat 4 times *ch 1, skip 1 st, 1 sc*, ch 1, skip 1 st, 1 inc, ch 1, skip 1 st, 1 sc, ch 1, skip 1 st, 1 inc, repeat 2 times *ch 1, skip 1 st, 1 sc*. (34 sts) DO NOT WORK THE LAST 2 STS (button placement).

✓ Place 4 markers in the center ch of the increases.

Rows 3-6: Ch 2 (pm in the ch space), repeat *1 sc in the ch from previous row, ch 1* across, making 1 increase at each of the 4 markers, and finish with 1 sc in the ch space with marker (Row 3 = 42 sts; Row 4 = 50 sts; Row 5 = 58 sts; and Row 6 = 66 sts).

Row 7: Ch 2 (pm in the ch space), repeat 4 times *1 sc in the ch from previous row, ch 1*, 1 sc in the marked ch [replace regular stitch marker with a green marker], ch 1 (pm, underarm), skip sts until next stitch marker [place a red marker on the 1st sc skipped (which is the 2nd sc of the inc)], 1 sc in the marked ch st, ch 1, repeat 9 times *1 sc in the ch st from previous row, ch 1*, 1 sc in the marked ch st, ch 1 (pm, underarm), skip the sts up to next marker [place a red marker in the 1st skipped sc (which is the 2nd sc of the inc)], 1 sc in the marked ch st [replace regular stitch marker with a green marker], repeat 4 times *ch 1, 1 sc in the ch st from previous row*. (42 sts) REMOVE the other 2 markers at increases.

✓ Red colored markers = **puffed sleeve version.**

✓ Green colored markers = **long-sleeved version.**

Then in the next row, continue with granite st, making 1 inc under the ch st at the 2 underarm markers, as follows:

Row 8: Ch 2 (pm in the ch space), repeat 4 times *1 sc under the ch from the previous row, ch 1*, 1 inc, repeat 10 times *ch 1, 1 sc under the ch from the previous row*, ch 1, 1 inc, repeat 5 times *ch 1, 1 sc under the ch from the previous row*. (46 sts)

Row 9: Ch 2 (pm in ch space), repeat *1 sc under the ch from previous row, ch 1*, working 1 inc in the 5th, 10th, 14th, and 19th sc, finish with 1 sc in the ch space with marker. (54 sts)

Row 10: Ch 2 (pm in ch space), *1 sc under the ch from the previous row, ch 1*, finish with 1 sc in the ch space with marker. (54 sts)

Rnd 11: Ch 2 (pm in ch space), repeat *1 sc under the ch from previous row, ch 1*. *Note: Be sure to end with ch 1 even if there is not a sc under it and close with a sl st in the ch space. (55 sts)* At this point, start to work in a spiral.

Rnd 12: Ch 1 (edge), 1 sc (pm) in the same ch-2 space, *ch 1, 1 sc under the ch from previous rnd*, (be sure to end with 1 sc under the ch before the connecting sl st) 1 sl st at the marker. (55 sts)

Rnd 13: Ch 2 (pm in the ch space), repeat *1 sc under the ch from previous rnd, ch 1*, sl st in the ch sp with marker. (55 sts)

Rnd 14: Repeat Rnd 12.

Rnd 15: Ch 2 (pm in the ch space), 1 inc, repeat 6 times *ch 1, 1 sc under the ch from the previous row*, ch 1, 1 inc, repeat 6 times *ch 1, 1 sc under the ch from the previous row*, ch 1, 1 inc, repeat 6 times *ch 1, 1 sc under the ch from the previous row*, ch 1, 1 inc, repeat 5 times *ch 1, 1 sc under the ch from the previous row*, ch 1, 1 sc in the ch space with marker. (63 sts)

Rnd 16: Ch 1 (edge), 1 sc (pm) in the same ch-2 space, repeat 31 times *ch 1, 1 sc under the ch from the previous rnd*, sl st at the marker. (63 sts)

Cut yarn.

Join yarn at end of neckline and ch 2, slip st, and fasten off to form buttonhole. Sew button on opposite side, at other end of the neckline.

Peter Pan Collar Version

Puffed Sleeves

Join mahogany (or blue) yarn at a red marker for sleeves.

Rnd 1: Ch 1 (edge), 1 sc (pm), ch 1, repeat 12 times *1 sc, ch 1 (not skipping any sts)*, 1 sc on the ch st from the inc at center of underarm (spread the sts a little to see the ch st better), ch 1, 1 sc at the marker.

Rnd 2: Ch 2 (pm in the ch space), repeat 13 times *1 sc under the ch from the previous rnd, ch 1*, 1 sc, 1 sl st in the ch space with marker.

Rnd 3: Ch 1 (edge), 1 sc in the ch space (pm), 13 sc under the ch sts *(Note: Not working any ch sts between the sc makes it possible to create decreases)*, sl st at the marker.

Rnd 4: Ch 1 (edge), repeat 4 times *sc2tog, 1 sc*, 1 sc, 1 sl st at the 1st dec.

Cut yarn. Make another identical sleeve.

STITCHES AND TECHNIQUES

- Chain stitch, slip stitch, single crochet: **see Stitches, page 34.**
- **Granite Stitch:** Repeat *1 sc in the ch-1 space, ch 1, skip 1 sc*.
- **Increase:** (sc, ch 1, sc) in the same st (only for Row 2) or in the same ch-1 space (for rest of rows). So, each inc adds 2 sts.
- The work is then done in the ch st of the inc.
- Chain stitch: **see Embroidery Stitches, page 38.**

  Notes: At the beginning of the row/rnd, the first 2 ch sts equal 1 edge st (which counts as 1 st in the total count between parentheses).
  On the rows, make the last sc in the initial ch-2 space of the previous row.

Peter Pan Collar

Join mustard (or dusty rose) yarn at the 1st unworked ch st on button side.

Row 1: Ch 1 (edge), 27 sc. (27 sts)

Row 2: Ch 1 to turn, 13 sc. (13 sts) DO NOT WORK OTHER STS.

Row 3: Ch 1 to turn, 1 sc, 2 sc in the same st, 11 sc (marker in the last sc). Cut yarn.

Skip 1 st (at center) from Row 1 and join yarn.

Row 2-b: Ch 1 (edge), 13 sc. (13 sts)

Row 3-b: Ch 1 to turn, 11 sc, 2 sc in the same st, 1 sc. Cut yarn.

For the edging, join yarn at the marker and ch 1 (= 1st sl st), 14 sl st, 2 sl st on the side of the rows, 1 sl st in the center st that was skipped, 2 sl st on the side of the rows, 14 sl sts. Cut yarn.

Pull mustard yarn through to back of sweater (to fasten down collar) and weave in ends.

Embroidered "Love" Version

Long Sleeves

Join brown yarn to a green marker for sleeves.

Rnd 1: Ch 2 (pm in ch space), repeat 6 times *1 sc under the ch st from previous row, ch 1*, 1 sc under the ch st from the inc (like at the beginning), ch 1, 1 sc under the ch st from the inc at middle of underarm (spread the sts a little to see the ch st better), ch 1, 1 sl st in the ch space with marker. Place marker at sl st and continue in spiral as follows: *1 sc under the ch st from previous rnd, ch 1* and continue until 3 in. (8 cm) from the marker.

Change yarn to beige for the edging on the last rnd.

Cut yarn. Make another identical sleeve.

"LOVE"

Place markers at ends of letters to form the word "love" (or any other word you choose up to 4 letters). Embroider each letter in chain st.

Striped Version

Follow the explanations for the basic body, but do not make sleeves and change colors every row or rnd.

EMPIRE SWEATER

INSTRUCTIONS

The number between parentheses is the number of sts at the end of the row (or rnd).

Note: Worked top down.

Body

With nude, and using 5 mm (US H-8) hook, chain 25 sts.

Row 1: 1 sc in the 2nd ch from hook, 23 sc. (24 sts)

Row 2: Repeat 6 times *1 inc, 3 dc*. (30 sts)

Row 3: Repeat 6 times *1 inc, 4 dc*. (36 sts)

SUPPLIES

· Bergère de France Pure Douceur yarn (#4 medium weight; 5% wool, 37% polyamide, 58% superkid mohair; 273 yd/250 m per 1.8 oz/50 g) in Peau (nude)

· Bergère de France Idéal yarn (#3 light weight; 30% acrylic, 30% polyamide, 40% combed wool; 136 yd/124 m per 1.8 oz/50 g) in Beige Rose (dusty rose)

· 3 small buttons

· 3.5 mm (US E-4) and 5 mm (US H-8) hooks

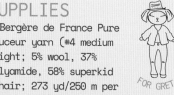

FOR GRETA

Row 4: Repeat 6 times *1 inc, 5 dc*. (42 sts)
✓ Place colored marker on the 7th, 15th, 29th, and 36th sts (and leave them for the sleeves).
Rnd 5 (divide for arms): 1 inc, 6 dc, skip 7 sts (= armhole), repeat 2 times *1 inc, 6 dc*, skip 7 sts (= armhole), 1 inc, 6 dc, close round with a sl st at marker. (32 sts)
Rnd 6: Repeat 32 times *3 dc in the same st*, sl st at the marker. (96 sts)
Rnd 7: 96 dc, sl st at the marker. (96 sts) Change to 3.5 mm (US E-4) hook and switch to dusty rose yarn at sl st.
Rnd 8: Ch 1 (= 1st sl st), 95 sl st, join with a sl st in the 1st ch st.
Cut yarn.

Sleeves

With nude, and using 5 mm (US H-8) hook, attach yarn at 2 colored markers at the same time.
Rnd 1: 1 dc, 1 inc, 6 dc, sl st at the marker. (9 sts)
Rnds 2-3: 9 dc, sl st at the marker. (9 sts)
Rnd 4: 9 inc, 1 sl st at the marker. (18 sts) Change to 3.5 mm (US E-4) hook and dusty rose yarn at the sl st.
Rnd 5: Ch 1 (= 1st sl st), 17 sl st, close with a sl st in the 1st ch st.
Cut yarn. Make another identical sleeve.

Buttonholes

In nude with 5 mm (US H-8) hook, join yarn to last stitch of neckline, on the right side of the opening, and then work in a single loop: ch 1, 1 sc in the same st, 1 sc on the side of Row 1, 2 sc on the side of the dc in Rows 2, 3, and 4, and then repeat in opposite direction on other side of opening (2 sc on the side of dc in Rows 2, 3, and 4, 1 sc in the side of Row 1, 1 sc in the last st of the neckline). Cut yarn.
Sew a button to the next-to-the-last sc, a second on the last one on that same side and center the last button between the other 2. Pass buttons between 2 sc on opposite side to button.

— SHORTS AND PANTS —

BOBBLE SHORTS

INSTRUCTIONS

The number between parentheses is the number of sts at the end of the rnd.

Note: Worked from the waist down.

STITCHES AND TECHNIQUES

· Chain stitch, slip stitch, single crochet, double crochet, double crochet increase: **see Stitches, page 34.**
· Changing colors: **see Techniques, page 39.**

Notes: Replace the 1st dc with ch 3 and pm in the 3rd ch of each row or rnd.

TIP

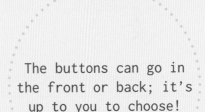

The buttons can go in the front or back; it's up to you to choose!

SUPPLIES

· Bergère de France Coton Fifty yarn (#2 fine weight; 4 ply; 50% cotton, 50% acrylic; 153 yd/140 m per 1.8 oz/50 g) in Perle (gray)
· 3.5 mm (US E-4) hook

FOR JO

STITCHES AND TECHNIQUES

· Chain stitch, slip stitch, single crochet, half double crochet, double crochet, front post double crochet: **see Stitches, page 34.**

· **Dc Bobble:** Repeat 4 times in the same st *yo, insert hook in the st, yo and pull through 2 loops*, yo and pull through all 5 loops. This is the same as dc 4 together in the same st.

Notes: The ch st at the beginning of the rnd is an edge st. Starting in Rnd 3, pm on the 1st sc (just after the ch st) or the 1st hdc (not indicated in the instructions).

SUPPLIES

· **Version A:** Bergère de France Coton Fifty yarn (#2 fine weight; 4 ply; 50% cotton, 50% acrylic; 153 yd/140 m per 1.8 oz/50 g) in Petrolier (dark blue); Mercerized cotton (100% Egyptian cotton; 617 yd/565 m per 3.5 oz/100 g) in White

· **Version B:** Bergère de France Coton Fifty yarn (#2 fine weight; 4 ply; 50% cotton, 50% acrylic; 153 yd/140 m per 1.8 oz/50 g) in Zan (black); Mercerized cotton (100% Egyptian cotton; 617 yd/565 m per 3.5 oz/100 g) in Ecru

· 1 small gray or silver button

· 3 mm (US C-2 or D-3) hook

FOR SALOME

FOR GRETA

Top of Shorts

Begin by chaining 54 sts and join to work in the round with a sl st in the 1st ch st.

Rnd 1: Ch 3 (= 1st dc), 53 dc, sl st in the 3rd ch. (54 sts)
Rnd 2: Ch 3 (= 1st dc), repeat 26 times *1 front post dc (fpdc), 1 dc*, sl st in the 3rd ch. (54 sts)

Note: It is possible to substitute regular dc for the front post dc.

From this point, stitches are worked in the round AND back and forth, as follows:

Rnd 3: Ch 1 to TURN, 1 sc in the sl st, repeat 8 times *1 bobble, 5 sc*, 1 bobble, 4 sc, sl st at the marker. (54 sts)
Rnd 4: Ch 1 to TURN, 1 hdc in the sl st, 53 hdc, sl st at the marker. (54 sts)
Rnd 5: Ch 1 to TURN, 1 sc in the sl st, 3 sc, repeat 8 times *1 bobble, 5 sc*, 1 bobble, 1 sc, sl st at the marker. (54 sts)
Rnd 6: Repeat Rnd 4.
Rnd 7: Repeat Rnd 3.
Rnd 8: Repeat Rnd 4.
Then separate the work to form legs.

First Leg

Rnd 9: Ch 1 to TURN, 1 sc in the sl st, 3 sc, repeat 3 times *1 bobble, 5 sc*, 1 bobble, 4 sc, sl st at the marker. (27 sts) DO NOT WORK OTHER STS.
Rnd 10: Ch 1 to TURN, 1 hdc in the sl st, 26 hdc, sl st at the marker. (27 sts)
Rnd 11: Ch 1 to TURN, 1 sc in the sl st, repeat 4 times *1 bobble, 5 sc*, 1 bobble, 1 sc, sl st at the marker. (27 sts)
Rnd 12: Ch 3 (= 1st dc), 26 dc, sl st at the marker. (27 sts) Cut yarn.

Second Leg

Attach yarn to the 1st st not worked from Rnd 8 and repeat Rnds 9–12. Cut yarn.

TORN JEANS

INSTRUCTIONS

The number between parentheses is the number of sts at the end of the rnd (or row).

Note: Worked from the bottom of the legs up to the waist.

First Leg

With dark blue (or black), chain 20 sts, and then work in a spiral starting in the 1st ch st:

Rnds 1–16: 20 sc. (20 sts)
Rnd 17: 10 sc, ch 4, skip 4 sts, 6 sc. (20 sts)
Rnd 18: 10 sc, 4 sc in the ch-4 space, 6 sc. (20 sts)
Rnds 19–24: 20 sc. (20 sts)
Rnd 25: 5 sc, 1 inc, 9 sc, 1 inc, 4 sc. (22 sts)
Rnd 26: 1 inc, 10 sc, 1 inc, 10 sc. (24 sts)
Rnds 27–28: 24 sc. (24 sts)
Rnd 29: 6 sc, 1 inc, 11 sc, 1 inc, 5 sc. (26 sts)

Rnds 30–31: 26 sc. (26 sts)

Rnd 32: Ch 1, 1 inc, repeat 2 times *8 sc, 1 inc*, 6 sc. (29 sts)

Rnds 33–34: 29 sc. (29 sts)

Rnd 35: 8 sc, 1 inc, repeat 2 times *9 sc, 1 inc*. (32 sts)

Rnd 36: 32 sc. (32 sts)

Rnd 37: 1 sc, 1 inc, repeat 2 times *10 sc, 1 inc*, 8 sc. (35 sts)

✓ During this rnd, place a colored marker on the 20th st. Cut yarn, leaving a long tail for sewing between the legs.

Second Leg

Work as for the first leg, but with no marker on Rnd 37. DO NOT CUT YARN.

Upper Jeans

Rnd 38: 3 sc (place colored marker in the next st), 35 sc on the 1st leg, starting at the colored marker, and then another 32 sc on the 2nd leg, starting at the colored marker. (70 sts)

Rnd 39: 18 sc, 1 invisible dec, 31 sc, 1 invisible dec, 17 sc. (68 sts)

Rnd 40: 68 sc. (68 sts)

Rnd 41: Repeat 4 times *15 sc, 1 invisible dec*. (64 sts)

Rnds 42–43: 64 sc. (64 sts)

Rnd 44: Repeat 2 times *8 sc, 1 invisible dec*, repeat 2 times **9 sc, 1 invisible dec**, 8 sc, 1 invisible dec, 9 sc, 1 invisible decrease, 1 sc. (58 sts)

Rnd 45: Repeat 2 times *1 invisible dec, 8 sc, 1 invisible dec, 7 sc, 1 invisible dec, 8 sc*. (52 sts)

Rnd 46: 52 sc, 1 sl st in the back loop at marker.

Rnd 47: Ch 3 (= 1st dc, pm on the 3rd ch), 51 dc in the back loop only, sl st at the marker. (52 sts)

Cut yarn.

FINISHING

Sew the button on the center stitch of the last rnd (= belt). Sew between the legs with yarn tail from 1st leg.

Back Pockets

Note: Worked from bottom point up.

With dark blue (or black), chain 2 sts, leaving a yarn tail at the beginning for sewing.

Row 1: Ch 1 in the 2nd ch (pm), 1 sc in the same st. (2 sts)

Row 2: Ch 1, 2 inc. (4 sts)

Row 3: Ch 1, 4 inc. (8 sts)

Rows 4–8: Ch 1, 8 sc. (8 sts)

Cut yarn, leaving a long tail.

Make another identical pocket.

With the jeans lying flat, place the pockets so the top edge of each pocket is below the loops not worked from Rnd 46. Space them out on Rnd 45 with 8 sts between them, 4 sts on either side of the center back. Sew them onto the jeans with the 2 strands of yarn (start and end of pocket). Then embroider around outside bottom edge in running stitch in white (or ecru).

STITCHES AND TECHNIQUES

· Chain stitch, slip stitch, single crochet, single crochet increase, invisible decrease, back loop only stitches: **see Stitches, page 34.**

· Working in a spiral: **see Techniques, page 39.**

· Running stitch, straight stitch: **see Embroidery Stitches, page 38.**

Note: Pm on the 1st sc of each rnd.

Embroidered Details

Zipper
With white (or ecru), embroider a zipper in running stitch as seen in photo on page 91.

Sides
With jeans flat, place a few markers down the sides of the legs. With white (or ecru), embroider seams in running stitch, going over 1 sc and then under 2 sc.

Knees
With white (or ecru), embroider large straight stitches to create the look of tears at the knees. Don't pull on the thread. Finish with a knot and cut thread on right side of work so it is visible.

Front Pockets
Put jeans on doll. With white (or ecru), embroider front pockets in running stitch starting between Rnds 3–4 of sc and going at a slant 3 rnds lower and 3 sc toward the outside.

Fold up the bottom edge to form a cuff.

FUZZY SHORTS

INSTRUCTIONS

The number between parentheses is the number of sts at the end of the rnd.

Waistband and Top of Shorts
With gray and the 4 mm (US G-6) hook, chain 40 sts and join to work in the round with sl st in the first ch.

Rnd 1: Ch 3 (pm in the 3rd ch), 39 dc, sl st at the marker, changing to pink yarn and 6 mm (US J-10) hook. (40 sts)

Rnd 2: Ch 3 (pm in the 3rd ch), 3 dc, dc2tog, repeat 5 times *4 dc, dc2tog*, 3 dc, working between each dc from previous rnd (*Note: Same for the following rnds*); don't work dc between the 1st and the last dc in gray, sl st at marker. (33 sts)

Rnd 3: Ch 3 (pm in the 3rd ch), 30 dc, dc2tog, sl st at marker. (32 sts) DO NOT CUT YARN.

First Leg
Rnds 4–5: Ch 3 (pm on the 3rd ch), 15 dc, sl st at the marker. (16 sts)

Note: Change to gray and 4 mm (US G-6) hook at the end of Rnd 5, at the sl st.

Rnd 6: Ch 1 (edge), repeat 8 times *1 sc, 2 sc in the same st*, sl st in the 1st sc.
Cut yarn.

Second Leg
Attach pink yarn at 1st st not worked in Rnd 3 and repeat Rnds 4–6.
Sew between legs with 2 small stitches.

SUPPLIES

· Bergère de France Plume yarn (#5 bulky weight; 11% combed wool, 42% acrylic, 47% polyamide; 87 yd/79.5 m per 1.8 oz/50 g) in Auréole (pink)

FOR SOPHIA

· Bergère de France Idéal yarn (#3 light weight; 30% acrylic, 30% polyamide, 40% combed wool; 136 yd/124 m per 1.8 oz/50 g) in Cendre (gray)
· 4 mm (US G-6) and 6 mm (US J-10) hooks

STITCHES AND TECHNIQUES
· Chain stitch, slip stitch, single crochet, double crochet, double crochet 2 together: **see Stitches, page 34.**
· Changing colors: **see Techniques, page 39.**

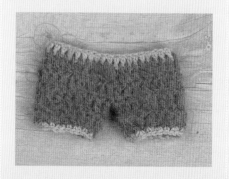

TEXTURED JOGGERS OR SHORTS

INSTRUCTIONS

The number between parentheses is the number of sts at the end of the rnd.

Upper Section for Both Versions

With gray, chain 54 sts and join to work in the round with sl st in the 1st ch.

Rnd 1: Ch 3, 53 dc, sl st at the marker. (54 sts)
Rnd 2: Ch 3, repeat 26 times *1 front post dc (fpdc), 1 dc*, 1 fpdc, sl st at the marker. (54 sts)
✓ Place colored marker at the 10th fpdc (= 20th st) and at the 18th fpdc (= 36th st).
Rnd 3: Ch 3, repeat 26 times *1 dc, 1 fpdc*, 1 dc, sl st at the marker. (54 sts)
Rnd 4: Repeat Rnd 2.
Rnd 5: Repeat Rnd 3. DO NOT CUT YARN.

First Leg

Rnd 6: Ch 3, (pm in 3rd ch), repeat 13 times *1 fpdc, 1 dc*, DO NOT WORK THE REMAINING STS, sl st at the marker. (27 sts)
Rnd 7: Ch 3, (pm in 3rd ch), repeat 13 times *1 dc, 1 fpdc*, sl st at the marker. (27 sts)

✓ **For the shorts:** Repeat Rnds 6–7 up to Rnd 10. DO NOT CUT YARN, and go to bottom band.
✓ **For the joggers:** Repeat Rnds 6–7 up to Rnd 16. DO NOT CUT YARN, and go to bottom band.

Bottom Band

Notes: Pm in the 1st st of each rnd.

Rnd 1: Ch 1, repeat 9 times *1 sc, sc2tog*, sl st at the marker. (18 sts)
Rnd 2: Ch 1, repeat 3 times *4 sc, sc2tog*, sl st at the marker. (15 sts)
Rnds 3–6: Ch 1, 15 sc, sl st at the marker.
Cut yarn.

Second Leg

Leaving a tail at the beginning for sewing seam between legs, join yarn to the 1st dc not worked in Rnd 5 and repeat starting in Rnd 6.

FINISHING

Using yarn from beginning of second leg, work 2 whipstitches to close seam between legs.

Pocket Details

With black yarn on needle on wrong side of work, bring up yarn next to colored marker and insert next to the dc, embroidering over another 3 sts in chain stitch, slanting down toward the outside.

SUPPLIES

· Bergère de France Coton Fifty yarn (#2 fine weight; 4 ply; 50% cotton, 50% acrylic; 153 yd/140 m per 1.8 oz/50 g) in Perle (gray) and a bit of Zan (black)
· 3 mm (US C-2 or D-3) hook

FOR ABBOTT

STITCHES AND TECHNIQUES

· Chain stitch, slip stitch, double crochet, front post double crochet: **see Stitches, page 34.**
· Joining with whipstitch: **see Techniques, page 39.**
· Chain stitch: **see Embroidery Stitches, page 36.**

Notes: For all rnds, pm in the 3rd ch of the 3 ch sts that count as the 1st dc.

TIP

"Classic" dc can be used throughout in place of front post stitches.

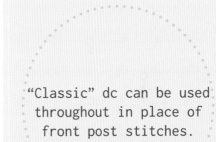

SUPPLIES

- Bergère de France Coton Fifty yarn (#2 fine weight; 4 ply; 50% cotton, 50% acrylic; 153 yd/140 m per 1.8 oz/50 g) in Gingembre (orange) and Turquoise, or (variation) Turquoise and Bengale (fuchsia)
- 3.5 mm (US E-4) hook

STITCHES AND TECHNIQUES

- Chain stitch, slip stitch, single crochet, half double crochet: **see Stitches, page 34.**
- **Special half double crochet:** With the half double crochet from the previous row facing you, insert hook in the loop directly below the top "V" loops.
- **Increase:** [1 sc, ch 1, 1 sc] under the same ch st. Each increase adds 2 sts.
- Joining with whipstitch: **see Techniques, page 39.**

Notes: For odd rows, start with a ch 2 and end with a ch 1. For even rows, start with 1 sc and end with 1 sc.

RIBBED BLOOMERS

INSTRUCTIONS

The number between parentheses is the number of sts at the end of the rnd (or row).

Waistband

With orange (or turquoise), ch 8 sts.
Rnd 1: 1 hdc in the 2nd ch, 6 hdc. (7 sts)
Rnds 2–36: Ch 1 (edge), 7 special hdc. (7 sts) DO NOT CUT YARN.
Joining: Ch 1, put the 2 ends edge to edge and join with 7 sc. This "seam" acts as a "rib" and will be at the center back of the bloomers.
Cut yarn.

Waistband and starting the top of bloomers

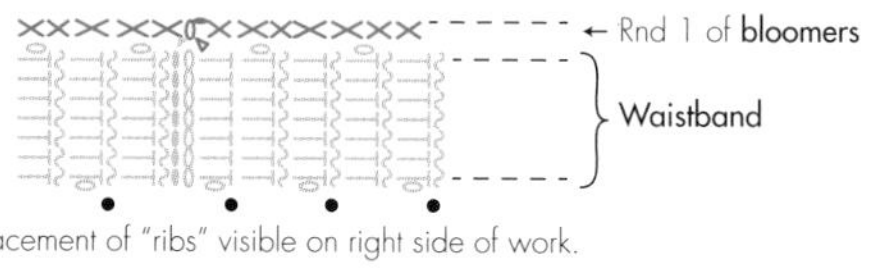

Placement of "ribs" visible on right side of work.

Key

- ◀ Cut yarn.
- ◁ Attach yarn.
- ○ **Chain 1:** Yo, pull through loop on the hook.
- : **1 slip stitch:** Insert hook in st, yo and draw through all loops on hook.
- × **1 single crochet:** Insert hook in st, yo and pull through the st, yo and pull yarn through all loops on the hook.
- T **1 half double crochet:** Yo, insert hook in st, yo and pull through the st, yo, draw through all loops on hook.
- T̃ **1 special half double crochet:** Work the hdc, inserting the hook in the loop directly below the top "V" loops of the hdc from the previous row.
- ▒ Turquoise
- ■ Fuchsia

Top of Bloomers

Join turquoise (or fuchsia) yarn at seam and work perpendicular to the waistband.
Rnd 1: Ch 1 (edge), 1 sc (pm), 2 sc, repeat 17 times *3 sc between each "rib"*, 1 sc, sl st at marker. (54 sts)
Rnd 2: Ch 1, 1 sc (pm), ch 1, skip 1 st, repeat 26 times *1 sc, ch 1, skip 1*, sl st at the marker. (54 sts)

Note: From this point on, the sc are worked under the ch sts.

Rnd 3: Ch 2 (pm in ch space), repeat 2 times *1 sc, ch 1*, 1 inc, repeat 8 times [repeat 2 times *ch 1, 1 sc*, ch 1, 1 inc], ch 1, 1 sl st in the ch space with marker. (72 sts)
Rnd 4: Ch 1, 1 sc (pm), ch 1, repeat 35 times *1 sc under the ch, ch 1*, 1 sc, sl st at the marker. (72 sts)
Rnd 5: Ch 2 (pm in ch space), repeat 2 times *1 sc under the ch, ch 1*, 1 inc, repeat 11 times [repeat 2 times **ch 1, 1 sc under the ch**, ch 1, 1 inc], ch 1, sl st in the ch space with marker. (96 sts)

Rnd 6: Ch 1, 1 sc (pm), repeat 48 times *ch 1, 1 sc under the ch*, sl st at the marker. (96 sts)

Rnd 7: Ch 2 (pm in the ch space), repeat 48 times *1 sc under the ch, ch 1*, sl st in the ch space with marker. (96 sts)

Rnd 8: Repeat Rnd 6.

Rnd 9: Ch 2 (pm in the ch space), repeat 5 times *1 sc under the ch, ch 1*, 1 inc, repeat 7 times [repeat 5 times **ch 1, 1 sc under the ch**, ch 1, 1 inc], ch 1, sl st in the ch space with marker. (112 sts)

Rnd 10: Ch 1, 1 sc in the ch space (pm), repeat 56 times *ch 1, 1 sc under the ch*, sl st at the marker. (112 sts) DO NOT CUT YARN.

First Leg

Rnd 11: Ch 2 (pm in the ch space), repeat 28 times *1 sc under the ch, ch 1*, sl st in the ch space with marker. (56 sts) DO NOT WORK REMAINING STS.

Rnd 12: Ch 1, 1 sc (pm), repeat 28 times *ch 1, 1 sc under the ch*, sl st at the marker. (56 sts)

Rnd 13: Repeat Rnd 11.

Rnd 14: Repeat Rnd 12.

Rnd 15: Ch 1, 1 sc (pm), repeat 28 times *1 sc under the ch*, sl st at the marker (leave it in place). (29 sts) Cut yarn.

Second Leg

Start at 1st unworked ch-1 space from Rnd 10 and work as for the previous leg starting in Rnd 11.

Work 2 whipstitches to sew seam between legs.

Leg Ribbing (x 2)

With orange (or turquoise), chain 5 sts.

Row 1: 1 hdc in the 2nd ch, 3 hdc, sl st at the leg marker.

Row 2: Ch 1 to turn, 4 special hdc. (Note: Do not work the previous sl st.)

Row 3: Ch 1 to turn, 4 special hdc, sl st at the leg, skipping 3 sts (see photo at right).

Rows 4-15: Repeat Rows 2-3.

Row 16: Ch 1 to turn, 4 special hdc.

Cut yarn, leaving a long tail for sewing.

Whipstitch together the 4 sts from Rnd 16 to the chain, inserting in the 3rd loop (as for the special hdc) and in the chain sts (see photo at right).

Make another identical leg ribbing and attach to bottom of the other leg as above.

SUPPLIES

- **Bib Overalls:** Bergère de France Coton Fifty yarn (#2 fine weight; 4 ply; 50% cotton, 50% acrylic; 153 yd/140 m per 1.8 oz/50 g) in the following colors: Berlingot (pink), Cytise (yellow), Turquoise, Perle (gray)
- **Shorts:** Bergère de France Coton Fifty yarn (#2 fine weight; 4 ply; 50% cotton, 50% acrylic; 153 yd/140 m per 1.8 oz/50 g) in Zan (black) and Coco (white)
- 3.5 mm (US E-4) and 5 mm (US H-8) hooks

FOR LOLY

FOR AVERY

STITCHES AND TECHNIQUES

- Magic circle, chain stitch, slip stitch, single crochet, double crochet: **see Stitches, page 34.**
- Joining with whipstitch: **see Techniques, page 39.**
- **Stripes for bib overalls:** Starting in Rnd 3, alternate *1 rnd pink, 1 rnd yellow, 1 rnd turquoise, 1 rnd gray*.
- **Stripes for shorts:** Starting in Rnd 3, alternate *1 rnd black, 1 rnd white*.

  Notes: Rnds 1–2 are in the same color.
  Replace the 1st dc with ch 3 and pm on the 3rd ch.

BIB OVERALLS OR SHORTS

INSTRUCTIONS

The number between parentheses is the number of sts at the end of the rnd.

Shorts (part used in all versions)

Note: Worked from waist down.

Waist

With pink for the overalls (or black for shorts) and 3.5 mm (US E-4) hook, chain 54 sts and join in the round with sl st in the 1st ch.

Rnd 1: Ch 1 (edge), 54 sc (pm in the 1st sc), sl st in the 1st sc. (54 sts)

Rnd 2 (same color as in Rnd 1): Repeat 18 times *3 dc in the same st, skip 2 sts*, sl st at the marker. (54 sts) Cut yarn.

Rnds 3–5: Repeat 18 times *3 dc between 2 groups of 3 dc from previous rnd*, sl st at the marker. (54 sts) Cut yarn.

First Leg

Rnds 6–8: Repeat 9 times *3 dc between 2 groups of 3 dc from previous rnd*, sl st at the marker. (27 sts) Cut yarn. DO NOT WORK OTHER STS.

Rnd 9: Ch 1 (edge), 27 sc, sl st at the marker, cut yarn.

Second Leg

Complete Rnds 6–9 starting from unworked sts in Rnd 5.
Sew seam between legs at the 3 center dc.
This completes the shorts.

Bib Overalls

Bib

With turquoise and with 3.5 mm (US E-4) hook, begin with a magic circle.

Rnd 1: Repeat 4 times *3 dc, ch 3*, sl st at the marker, ch 1, cut yarn.

Key

◀ Cut yarn.

◁ Attach yarn.

◯ Magic circle

∘ **Chain 1:** Yo, pull through loop on the hook.

- **1 single crochet:** Insert hook in st, yo and pull through the st, yo and pull yarn through all loops on the hook.

┬ **1 double crochet:** Yo then insert hook in st, yo and pull through st, and then repeat *yo, pull through 2 loops*.

▨ Turquoise

▢ Yellow

▧ Pink

Granny Square Bib

Rnd 2 (yellow): Join yarn in a ch-3 space, repeat 4 times *3 dc, ch 3, and 3 dc in the ch space*, sl st at the marker, ch 1, cut yarn.

Rnd 3 (pink): Join yarn in a ch-3 space, repeat 4 times *[3 dc, ch 3, and 3 dc] in the ch space, 3 dc between the 2 groups of 3 dc*, sl st at the marker, ch 1, cut yarn.

Sew together the **bib** and the **shorts**, right side to right side, using whipstitch, centering the granny square on the front of the shorts.

Straps

Join 2 yarns together in a ch-3 space in a corner of the granny square with 5 mm (US H-8) hook, ch 25 sts, join with 1 sl st at the back between 2 groups of 3 dc on the opposite side (to cross the straps).
Repeat these steps for the second strap, spacing them 6 groups of 3 dc apart on the **back**.

—
SKIRTS
—

RIBBED SKIRT

INSTRUCTIONS

The number between parentheses is the number of sts at the end of the row.

Skirt

With pink, ch 17 sts.
Row 1: 1 hdc in the 2nd ch, 15 hdc. (16 sts)
Rows 2-54: To make the waistband, ch 1, 16 special hdc. (16 sts)
Turn a quarter turn, and then work on the long side as follows:
Row 1: Ch 1, 2 sc between each "rib." (54 sts)
Row 2: Ch 3 (= 1st dc), 53 dc. (54 sts)
DO NOT CUT YARN, ch 1 and seam together the open edges of the skirt with loose sc.
Cut yarn.

Cord

With turquoise, ch 115 sts, cut yarn. Weave this cord through the top row of dc, starting at the front middle (with the seam at center of back), and repeating around *insert cord to left behind 3 dc and then over 1 dc*.

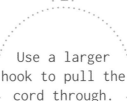

TIP

Use a larger hook to pull the cord through.

SUPPLIES

• Bergère de France Coton Fifty yarn (#2 fine weight; 4 ply; 50% cotton, 50% acrylic; 153 yd/140 m per 1.8 oz/50 g) in Berlingot (pink) and Turquoise
• 3.5 mm (US E-4) hook

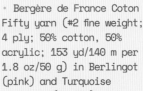
FOR JOSETTE

STITCHES AND TECHNIQUES

• Chain stitch, single crochet, half double crochet, double crochet: **see Stitches, page 34.**
• **Special half double crochet:** With the half double crochet from the previous row facing you, insert hook in the loop directly below the top "V" loops.

SUPPLIES

· **Version A:** Bergère de France Idéal yarn (#3 light weight; 30% acrylic, 30% polyamide, 40% combed wool; 136 yd/124 m per 1.8 oz/50 g) in Girolle (mustard); Mercerized cotton (100% Egyptian cotton; 617 yd/565 m per 3.5 oz/100 g) in white and black

· **Version B (stripes):** Bergère de France Idéal yarn (#3 light weight; 30% acrylic, 30% polyamide, 40% combed wool; 136 yd/124 m per 1.8 oz/50 g) in Everest (white), Beige Rose (dusty rose); Mercerized cotton (100% Egyptian cotton; 617 yd/565 m per 3.5 oz/100 g) in black; Bergère de France Metalika yarn (38% polyamide, 62% metal-effect polyester; 710 yd/649 m per 0.9 oz/25.5 g) in Etoile (gold) (optional, for some shine)

· 4 mm (US G-6) hook

FOR HYACINTH & ROSEMARY

STITCHES AND TECHNIQUES

· Chain stitch, slip stitch, double crochet, double crochet increase: **see Stitches, page 34.**

· Changing colors: **see Techniques, page 39.**

Notes: Replace 1st dc with ch 3 and pm on the 3rd ch.

For version A: Starting in Rnd 2, work the even rnds holding mustard and white together and work odd rnds in mustard. So at the end of Rnd 1 and each odd rnd, add white at the sl st; at the end of each even rnd, leave white on hold on wrong side of work at the sl st.

For version B: Work odd rnds with white and gold yarn held together and even rnds in dusty rose.

SCALLOPED-HEM SKIRT

INSTRUCTIONS

The number between parentheses is the number of sts at the end of the rnd (or row).

Note: Worked from top to bottom.

With mustard (or white), ch 48 sts, join to work in the round with a sl st in the 1st ch.

Rnds 1-2: 48 dc, sl st at the marker. (48 sts)

Rnd 3: Repeat 6 times *7 dc, 1 inc*, sl st at the marker. (54 sts)

Rnd 4: 54 dc. (54 sts)

Rnd 5: Repeat 6 times *8 dc, 1 inc*, sl st at the marker. (60 sts)

Rnd 6: Ch 1 (pm), skip 3 sts (including the 1st), repeat 10 times *5 dc in the same st, skip 2 sts, sl st, skip 2 sts*, sl st at the marker.

Cut yarns.

FINISHING

Weave a thread (in black here) through Rnd 1, starting in the middle of the front and alternating over and then under 2 dc. Put skirt on the doll before tying knot to be sure it is not too tight.

STRIPED SKIRT

INSTRUCTIONS

The number between parentheses is the number of sts at the end of the row (or rnd).

Skirt

With orange, ch 17 sts.

Row 1: 1 sc in the 2nd ch from hook, 15 sc. (16 sts)

Row 2: Ch 1 to turn, 16 sc. (16 sts) Switch to white at last yo of the last sc. DO NOT CUT ORANGE YARN.

Row 3: Ch 1 to turn, 16 sc. (16 sts) Switch to orange during last yo of the last st. DO NOT CUT WHITE YARN.

Rows 4–88: Repeat Rows 2–3 in Stripe pattern, changing color after each Row 2, ending with 44 stripes. DO NOT CUT YARN.

ASSEMBLY

Ch 1 and join the 16 sts of the sides together with sc. Cut yarn and turn work over (the sc used to seam must be turned to wrong side of skirt).

Waistband

Join white yarn at the end of an orange stripe.

Rnd 1: Ch 1 (edge), 1 sc, repeat 21 times *2 sc at end of a white stripe, 1 sc at end of an orange stripe*, 2 sc at the end of a white stripe, sl st at the marker. (66 sts)

Rnd 2: Ch 1, 8 sc, sc2tog, repeat 5 times *8 sc, sc2tog*, 6 sc, sl st at the marker. (60 sts)

Rnd 3: Ch 1, 4 sc, sc2tog, repeat 9 times *4 sc, sc2tog*, sl st at the marker. (50 sts)

Rnd 4: Ch 1, 4 sc, sc2tog, repeat 7 times *4 sc, sc2tog*, 2 sc, sl st at the marker. (42 sts) Cut yarn.

Bottom Edging

Join orange yarn at the end of an orange stripe (then work stitches on top of and encircling the yarn carried up the side).

Rnd 1: Ch 1 (edge), 1 sc, 4 sc in the same st, repeat 21 times *1 sl st at end of a white stripe, 5 sc at the end of an orange stripe*, 1 sl st at the end of white stripe, sl st at the marker.

Cut yarn.

Buttons (optional)

On one vertical stripe, evenly space out 4 buttons (see photo).

SUPPLIES

- Bergère de France Coton Fifty yarn (#2 fine weight; 4 ply; 50% cotton, 50% acrylic; 153 yd/140 m per 1.8 oz/50 g) in Coco (white) and Gingembre (orange)
- 4 small buttons or beads (optional)
- 3.5 mm (US E-4) hook

STITCHES AND TECHNIQUES

- Chain stitch, slip stitch, single crochet, single crochet 2 together: **see Stitches, page 34.**
- Changing colors: **see Techniques, page 39.**
- **Stripes:** Alternate 2 rows in orange and 2 rows in white.

Notes: Carry yarns up the side; they will be hidden in the edging.

Pm on the 1st sc of each row (not indicated in the instructions). The ch st at the beginning of the row or rnd is an edge st that is used only to turn the work.

SUPPLIES

· Bergère de France Coton Fifty yarn (#2 fine weight; 4 ply; 50% cotton, 50% acrylic; 153 yd/140 m per 1.8 oz/50 g) in Perle (gray)
· Piece of soft tulle (so it falls nicely)
· 4 mm (US G-6) hook

FOR VIOLET

STITCHES AND TECHNIQUES

· Chain stitch, slip stitch, single crochet, double crochet: see **Stitches, page 34.**
· Fringe: see **Techniques, page 39.**

Insert hook in unworked sts.

NO-SEW TULLE TUTU

INSTRUCTIONS

The number between parentheses is the number of sts at the end of the rnd (or row).

Waistband

Begin by chaining 48 sts and join to work in the round with sl st in the 1st ch.

Rnd 1 (waist): Ch 3 (pm in the 3rd ch), 47 dc, sl st at the marker. (48 sts)

Rnd 2 (base to which the tulle is attached): Ch 1 (pm), repeat 24 times *1 sc, ch 3, skip 1 st*, sl st at the marker. Remove hook from the loop, put a marker in the loop, and then keep on hold.

Tulle Skirt

Cut 24 strips approximately 3 × 8 in/8 × 20 cm (it's not important if they're not completely straight).

Attaching to Waistband

Attach the strips of tulle like fringe to each ch-3 space from Rnd 2.

Note: Use the thumb and index finger to pull the ends of the tulle through the loop. Be sure to completely tighten a fringe only when the next fringe is in place.

Remove marker from the waistband loop and return hook to the loop.

Rnd 3 (scalloped edging): WORKING ONLY IN THE SKIPPED STS FROM RND 2, ch 1 (pm), sl st in the 1st skipped st from Rnd 1, repeat 24 times *1 sc, ch 5, 1 sl st, ch 5, 1 sc in the same skipped st, ch 1, skip the sc from the previous rnd*, sl st at the marker.
Cut yarn.

Even out bottom edge of the tulle if needed.

ZIGZAG SKIRT

INSTRUCTIONS

The number between parentheses is the number of sts at the end of the rnd.

Note: Worked from bottom up.

Skirt

With turquoise, ch 72 sts and join to work in the round with a sl st in the 1st ch.

Rnd 1: Repeat 6 times *1 V, 4 dc, 1 double dec, 4 dc*, 1 sl st in the 4-ch space, switching to white at the last ch st. (72 sts) KEEP TURQUOISE YARN ON HOLD.

SUPPLIES

· Bergère de France Coton Fifty yarn (#2 fine weight; 4 ply; 50% cotton, 50% acrylic; 153 yd/140 m per 1.8 oz/50 g) in Turquoise and Coco (white)
· 3.5 mm (US E-4) hook

FOR DOMI

Rnds 2–7: Repeat 5 times *1 V in the ch-1 space, 4 dc, 1 double dec, 4 dc*, 1 V in the ch-1 space, 4 dc, 1 double dec, 2 dc, 1 inc, 1 sl st in the ch-4 space, changing colors. (72 sts)

Rnd 8: Ch 1, 1 sc, in the ch space (pm), 1 sl st in the ch space, 1 sc in the ch space, repeat 6 times *2 hdc, 2 dc, 1 tr, 2 dc, 2 hdc, 1 sc, 1 sl st (on the ch st), 1 sc*, sl st at the marker. (72 sts) ONLY CUT TURQUOISE YARN.

Waistband

Rnd 9 (white): Ch 1 (edge), repeat 24 times *1 sc, sc2tog*, 1 sl st in the 1st sc. (48 sts)

Rnd 10 (white): Ch 1, repeat 8 times *4 sc, sc2tog*, 1 sl st in the 1st sc. (40 sts)

Cut yarn.

STITCHES AND TECHNIQUES

· Chain stitch, slip stitch, single crochet, half double crochet, double crochet, triple crochet, single crochet 2 together, double crochet increase: **see Stitches, page 34.**

· **1 V:** [1 dc, ch 1, and 1 dc] in the same st.

· For the 1st V of each rnd, work: [ch 4 (= 1st dc + ch 1) and 1 dc] in the same st.

· **Double Decrease:** Double crochet 3 together.

· Changing colors: **see Techniques, page 39.**

Note: Work the odd rnds in turquoise and the even rnds in white.

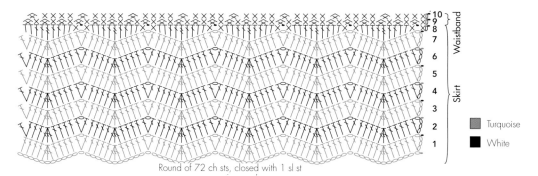

Round of 72 ch sts, closed with 1 sl st

10
9
8
7
6 Waistband
5
4 Skirt
3
2
1

▇ Turquoise
■ White

Key

◀ Cut yarn.

⊙ **Chain 1:** Yo, pull through loop on the hook.

‒ **1 slip stitch:** Insert hook in st, yo and pull through all loops on the hook.

× **1 single crochet:** Insert hook in st, yo and pull through the st, yo and pull through all loops on the hook.

T **1 half double crochet:** Yo, insert hook in st, yo and pull through the st, yo, draw through all loops on hook.

Ŧ **1 double crochet:** Yo then insert hook in st, yo and pull through st, and then repeat *yo, pull through 2 loops*.

Ŧ **1 triple crochet:** 2 yo then insert hook in st, yo and pull through st, and then repeat *yo, pull through 2 loops*.

⌃ **1 single crochet 2 together:** Insert hook in st, yo and pull through st, and then repeat this step in the next st, yo and pull through all loops on hook at once.

Ѫ **1 double decrease (= dc3tog):** Work 3 incomplete dc (leave last loop on hook), and then yo and pull through all 4 loops on hook.

SUPPLIES

- Bergère de France Coton Fifty yarn (#2 fine weight; 4 ply; 50% cotton, 50% acrylic; 153 yd/140 m per 1.8 oz/50 g) in the following colors: Bengale (fuchsia), Berlingot (pink), Coco (white)
- 3.5 mm (US E-4) hook

STITCHES AND TECHNIQUES

- Chain stitch, slip stitch, working in the back loop only, double crochet, back post double crochet: **see Stitches, page 34.**

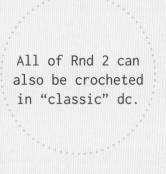

TIP

All of Rnd 2 can also be crocheted in "classic" dc.

SUPPLIES

- Your choice of fabric
- Sewing needle and thread (or machine)
- Narrow flat elastic band
- Safety pin

FOR FAWNTINE FOR ANNA FOR NINA

RUFFLED SKIRT

INSTRUCTIONS

The number between parentheses is the number of sts at the end of the rnd.

Base

Note: Worked from the waist down.

With fuchsia, ch 53 sts (pm in the last ch).
Rnd 1: 1 dc in the 5th ch from hook, 48 dc, sl st at the marker. (50 sts)
Rnd 2: Ch 3 (pm in the 3rd ch), repeat 24 times *1 back post dc (bpdc), 1 dc*, 1 dc, sl st at the marker. (50 sts)
Rnd 3: Ch 1 (edge), 1 sc in back loop (place colored marker in the unworked front loop), 49 sc in back loop only, sl st at the marker. (50 sts)
Rnd 4: Ch 3 (pm in the 3rd ch), repeat 24 times *1 dc, ch 1, skip 1 st*, 1 dc, sl st at the marker. (50 sts)
Rnd 5: Ch 3 (pm in the 3rd ch), repeat 24 times *1 dc, 1 dc under the ch st*, 1 dc, sl st at the marker. (50 sts)
Rnds 6-11: Repeat Rnds 3-5.
Cut yarn.

Note: There should be 3 colored markers in all.

Ruffles

Join fuchsia yarn at the last colored marker (in Rnd 9).
Rnd 1 (only in the front loop of previous unworked sts): Ch 3 (pm in the 3rd ch), 2 dc in the same st, repeat 49 times *3 dc in the same st*, sl st at the marker. (150 sts)
Rnd 2: Ch 3 (pm in the 3rd ch), 149 dc. (150 sts)
Cut yarn.
Then repeat Rnds 1-2 in pink at the middle colored marker (of Rnd 6).
Then repeat Rnds 1-2 in white at the top colored marker (of Rnd 3).

FABRIC SKIRT

INSTRUCTIONS

1. With the fabric, cut a rectangle to the desired size.
2. Fold in half, right sides together, and sew side seam to close the skirt.
3. At the top, fold fabric down ¾ in/2 cm toward the inside, and sew all around edge, leaving an opening of about 1 in/2.5 cm.

Note: Don't hem the bottom; this will give it a "frayed" look.

4. Fasten safety pin on end of elastic band and slide it through the top casing.

5. Sew the 2 ends of the elastic together, adjusting the skirt on the doll.

6. Sew the opening closed.

DRESSES, SUMMER WEAR & MORE

—

WINTER DRESS

INSTRUCTIONS

The number between parentheses is the number of sts at the end of the row (or rnd).

Top

Note: Worked from the neckline down to the waist.

With dusty rose, ch 34 sts.

Row 1: 1 sc in the 2nd ch from hook, 32 sc. (33 sts)

Row 2: Ch 1 to turn, repeat 15 times *1 V in the same st, skip 1 st*, 1 V in the same st, DO NOT WORK THE LAST ST (= placement of snap). (16 ch-2 spaces)

Row 3: Ch 1 to turn, repeat 4 times *1 inc in ch-2 space, 3 V*. Switch to beige in the last st.

Row 4: Ch 1, repeat 4 times *1 inc, 4 V*. Switch to dusty rose in the last st.

Row 5: Ch 1, repeat 8 times *1 inc, 2 V*.

Row 6: Ch 1, 32 V. Switch to beige in the last st.

Rnd 7: Ch 1, 5 V, skip 6 groups of ch spaces (= arms), 10 V, skip 6 groups of ch spaces (= arms), 5 V, join to work in round with a sl st in the 1st sc. Switch to dusty rose in the sl st.

Rnds 8-9: Ch 1, 20 V, sl st in the 1st sc. Switch to beige in the last sl st and cut dusty rose yarn only.

Skirt

Rnd 10: Repeat 16 times *1 dc in the 1st sc of the V, 1 dc in the ch space*, sl st at the marker.

Rnd 11: Repeat 10 times *3 dc, [1 dc and 1 front post dc] in the next st*, sl st at the marker. (50 sts)

Rnd 12: Repeat 10 times *4 dc, [1 dc and 1 front post dc] in the next st*, sl st at the marker. (60 sts)

SUPPLIES

· Bergère de France Idéal yarn (#3 light weight; 30% acrylic, 30% polyamide, 40% combed wool; 136 yd/124 m per 1.8 oz/50 g) in Meije (beige) and Beige Rose (dusty rose)

· 1 snap

· 4 mm (US G-6) hook

FOR AGATHA

STITCHES AND TECHNIQUES

· Magic circle, chain stitch, slip stitch, single crochet, double crochet, front post double crochet, triple crochet: **see Stitches, page 34.**

· **1 V:** [1 sc, ch 2, and 1 sc] in the same st (only for Row 2) or in the ch-2 space of the previous row or rnd.

· Changing colors, working in a spiral: **see Techniques, page 39.**

Notes for top:
Increase: [1 sc, ch 2, 1 sc, ch 2, and 1 sc] in the same ch-2 space from previous row.
Stripes: 3 rows in dusty rose, 1 row in beige, 2 rows in dusty rose, 1 rnd in beige, 2 rnds in dusty rose. Note: Do not cut the yarn when changing colors.
The ch st at beginning of row/rnd is an edge stitch used only to turn the work.

Note for the skirt: Replace the 1st dc with ch 3 and pm on the 3rd ch at beginning of each rnd (not indicated in the instructions).

SUPPLIES
· Bergère de France Pure Douceur yarn (#4 medium weight; 5% wool, 37% polyamide, 58% superkid mohair; 273 yd/250 m per 1.8 oz/50 g) in Peau (nude)
· 3 small buttons
· Ribbon
· 3.5 mm (US E-4) hook
· Matching sewing thread and needle
· Safety pin

FOR PIKI

Rnd 13: Repeat 10 times *5 dc, [1 dc and 1 front post dc (fpdc)] in the next st*, sl st at the marker. (70 sts)

Rnd 14: Repeat 10 times *6 dc [1 dc and 1 fpdc] in the next st*, sl st at the marker. (80 sts)

Rnd 15: Repeat 10 times *7 dc, [1 dc and 1 fpdc] in the next st*, sl st at the marker. (90 sts)

Rnds 16-17: Repeat 10 times *8 dc, 1 fpdc*, sl st at the marker. (90 sts) Switch to dusty rose in the sl st at end of the rnd.

Rnd 18: Ch 1, repeat 10 times *1 sc, 2 hdc, 2 dc, 2 hdc, 1 sc, 1 sl st in the front post dc*, ch 1 to join and cut yarns.

¾ Sleeves (optional)

On the right side, join dusty rose yarn in the 1st ch space next to underarm.

Rnd 1 (pm in the 1st sc): Ch 1, 6 V, sl st at the marker.

Rnds 2-9 (in spiral): 6 V.

Finish with a sl st in the 1st sc of Rnd 9, ch 1 to join and cut yarn.

Follow same steps on other sleeve.

FINISHING

Bow

With dusty rose, start with a magic circle.

Rnd 1: Repeat 2 times *ch 4, 4 tr, ch 4, sl st in the circle*. Cut yarn, leaving a long tail. Wind tail around the center, and then tie knot with yarn tail from beginning. Attach bow to back by bringing yarn tails around sides of a st, tie 2 knots on back and weave in ends.

Sew the two parts of the snap to the 1st and last sts of Row 1.

"SOFT AND SWEET" DRESS

INSTRUCTIONS

The number between parentheses is the number of sts at the end of the row (or rnd).

Dress

Note: Worked from top to bottom.

Start by chaining 32 sts (pm in the last st).

Row 1: 1 dc in the 5th ch from hook, 27 dc. (29 sts)

Row 2: Repeat 9 times *2 dc, 1 back post dc*, 2 dc. (29 sts)

Row 3: Repeat 9 times *1 inc, 1 dc, 1 front post dc*, 2 dc. (38 sts)

Row 4: Repeat 9 times *1 inc, 2 dc, 1 back post dc*, 2 dc. (47 sts)

Row 5: Repeat 9 times *1 inc, 3 dc, 1 front post dc*, 2 dc. (56 sts)

✓ Place colored markers on the 12th dc and the 41st dc and leave them there (= placement of cap sleeves).

Row 6: Repeat 2 times *5 dc, 1 back post dc*, [ch 3, skip 6 sts] (= underarm), repeat 3 times *5 dc, 1 back post dc*, 5 dc [ch 3, skip 6 sts] (= underarm), repeat 2 times *1 back post dc, 5 dc*. (53 sts)

Rnd 7: Repeat 2 times *5 dc, 1 front post dc*, 3 dc in the 3 ch sts, repeat 3 times *5 dc, 1 front post dc*, 5 dc, 3 dc in the 3 ch sts, repeat 2 times *1 front post dc, 5 dc*, close the round with sl st at the marker. (53 sts)

Rnd 8: 53 dc, sl st at the marker (place colored marker in 1 dc of this row). (53 sts)

Rnd 9: 53 inc, sl st at the marker. (106 sts)

Rnd 10: 106 tr, sl st at the marker. (106 sts)

Rnd 11: 106 dc, sl st at the marker. (106 sts)

Rnd 12: 106 tr, sl st at the marker. (106 sts)

Rnd 13: Repeat Rnd 11.

Rnd 14: Repeat Rnd 12.

Cut yarn.

Cap Sleeve

Join yarn at a marker in Row 5 and repeat 4 times *1 inc, 3 dc in the next st*. Cut yarn.

Follow same steps on other shoulder.

FINISHING

Sew buttons to the 1st dc of Rows 1, 4, and 7 on right side. Slide the buttons between the 1st and 2nd dc of the opposite side to button.

Fasten safety pin to end of ribbon and slide it through Row 8 (use marker to find right Row), starting at front center, and repeat all the way around *go under 3 dc and then over 1 dc*, bring up in same space and tie a bow.

STITCHES AND TECHNIQUES

· Chain stitch, slip stitch, double crochet, front and back post double crochet, double crochet increase, triple crochet: **see Stitches, page 34.**

Notes: Starting in Row 2, replace 1st dc with ch 3 or the 1st tr with ch 4 and pm on the 3rd (or 4th) ch to mark the beginning of the row/rnd.

Odd rows are on the right side of the work (all dc post sts appear raised on front of work).

SUPPLIES

- Bergère de France Coton Fifty yarn (#2 fine weight; 4 ply; 50% cotton, 50% acrylic; 153 yd/140 m per 1.8 oz/50 g) in the following colors: Berlingot (pink), Bengale (fuchsia), Coquille (peach beige)
- 1 small snap
- 3.5 mm (US E-4) hook

STITCHES AND TECHNIQUES

- Chain stitch, single crochet, double crochet, double crochet increase: see **Stitches, page 34.**
- **1 V:** 2 dc in the middle of a group of 2 dc from the previous row (starting in Row 3).
- **Double Increase:** 3 dc in the middle of a group of 2 dc from the previous row. In next row, work between the 1st and 2nd dc (= 1st middle) and then the 2nd and 3rd dc (= 2nd middle).
- Changing colors: see **Techniques, page 39.**

CANDY PINK DRESS

INSTRUCTIONS

The number between parentheses is the number of sts at the end of the rnd (or row).
To make the yoke and beginning of the skirt, refer to diagram on page 107.

Yoke

With fuchsia, ch 33 sts.
Row 1: Ch 1 in the 2nd chain from hook (pm), 31 sc. (32 sts)
Row 2: Join pink yarn at the marker, [ch 3 (= 1st dc) and 1 V] in the same st (pm between the ch 3 and the 1st dc), repeat 3 times *repeat 4 times **skip 1 st, 1V**, skip 1 st, 1 double inc*. (36 sts)
Cut yarn.

Note: Don't work the last st (= placement of snap).

Row 3: Join fuchsia yarn at the marker, [ch 3 (= 1st dc) and 1 dc] in the same space (pm between the ch 3 and the 1st dc), 1 V, repeat 3 times *1 double inc, 4 V*, 1 double inc, 2 V. (44 sts) Cut yarn.
Row 4: Join pink yarn at the marker, [ch 3 (1st dc) and 2 dc] in the same st (pm between the ch 3 and the 1st dc), 6 V, 1 double inc, 8 V, 1 double inc, 6 V, 1 double inc. (52 sts) Cut yarn.
Row 5 (divide for arms): Join fuchsia yarn at the marker, [ch 3 (= 1st dc) and 1 dc] in the same space (pm between the ch 3 and the 1st dc), 4 V, skip [3 V and the double inc] (= arms), 8 V, skip [the double inc and 3 V] (= arms), 5 V. (36 sts) Cut yarn.
Row 6: Join pink yarn at the marker, [ch 3 (= 1st dc) and 1 dc] in the same st, (pm between the ch 3 and the 1st dc), 17 V. (36 sts) Cut yarn.
Rnd 7: Join fuchsia yarn at the marker, [ch 3 (= 1st dc) and 1 dc] in the same stitch (pm between the ch 3 and the 1st dc), 17 V (= 36 sts), sl st at the marker. Switch to pink at the sl st.
Rnd 8: [Ch 3 (= 1st dc) and 1 dc] in the same st, (pm between the ch 3 and the 1st dc), 17 V (= 36 sts), sl st at the marker. Change color when working sl st at end of rnd, BUT DO NOT CUT THE YARN.

Checked Pattern Skirt

Rnd 9: Ch 1, 1 sc (pm) and 1 sc in the same st, repeat 35 times *2 sc in the same st*, sl st at the marker, switching to beige. (72 sts) Leave the fuchsia yarn on hold on wrong side.
Rnd 10: Ch 3 (= 1st dc, pm in the 3rd ch), 3 dc, ch 3, repeat 8 times *skip 4 sts, 4 dc, ch 3*, sl st at the marker (leave it in place), cut yarn.

Rnd 11: Join pink yarn to the 1st skipped st of Rnd 9; work in the dc from Rnd 9, working over and encircling the ch sts from Rnd 10, ch 3 (= 1st dc, pm in the 3rd ch), 3 dc, ch 3, repeat 8 times *skip 4 sts, 4 dc, ch 3*, sl st at the marker (leave it in place), cut yarn.

Rnd 12: Picking up fuchsia yarn, ch 3 at the marker from Rnd 10; work in the dc from Rnd 10, encircling the ch sts from Rnd 11, ch 3 (= 1st dc, pm in the 3rd ch), 3 dc, ch 3, repeat 8 times *skip 4 sts, 4 dc, ch 3*, sl st at the marker (leave it in place), cut yarn.

Rnd 13: Join beige yarn at the Rnd 11 marker; work in the dc from Rnd 11, encircling the ch sts from Rnd 12, ch 3 (= 1st dc, pm in the 3rd ch), 3 dc, ch 3 repeat 8 times *skip 4 sts, 4 dc, ch 3*, sl st at the marker (leave it in place), cut yarn.

Rnd 14 (beginning of increases): Join pink yarn at marker from Rnd 12; work in the dc from Rnd 12, encircling the ch sts from Rnd 13, ch 3 (= 1st dc, pm in the 3rd ch), 2 inc, 1 dc, ch 3, repeat 8 times *skip 4 sts, 1 dc, 2 inc, 1 dc, ch 3*, sl st at the marker (leave it in place), cut yarn.

Rnd 15: Join fuchsia yarn at the Rnd 13 marker; work in the dc from Rnd 13, encircling the ch sts from Rnd 14, ch 3 (= 1st dc, pm in the 3rd ch), 2 inc, 1 dc, ch 5, repeat 8 times *skip 6 sts, 1 dc, 2 inc, 1 dc, ch 5*, sl st at the marker (leave it in place), cut yarn.

Rnd 16: Join beige yarn at the marker from Rnd 14; work in the dc from Rnd 14, encircling the ch sts from Rnd 15, ch 3 (= 1st dc, pm in the 3rd ch), 5 dc, ch 5, repeat 8 times *skip 6 sts, 6 dc, ch 5*, sl st at the marker (leave it in place), cut yarn.

Rnds 17–20: Same as Rnd 16 in pink, fuchsia, beige, and then pink. *Note: At the end of Rnd 20, switch to fuchsia at the sl st.*

Rnd 21: Ch 1, repeat 8 times *6 sc, 6 dc encircling the ch sts from the previous rnd*, sl st in the 1st ch. Cut yarn.

Sew the two parts of the snap to the 1st and last sts of Row 1.

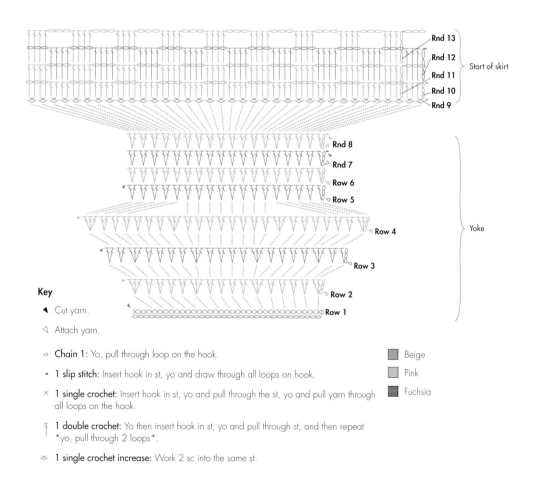

Key

◀ Cut yarn.

◁ Attach yarn.

◡ **Chain 1:** Yo, pull through loop on the hook.

– **1 slip stitch:** Insert hook in st, yo and draw through all loops on hook.

× **1 single crochet:** Insert hook in st, yo and pull through the st, yo and pull yarn through all loops on the hook.

┬ **1 double crochet:** Yo then insert hook in st, yo and pull through st, and then repeat *yo, pull through 2 loops*.

⋙ **1 single crochet increase:** Work 2 sc into the same st.

▨ Beige

▨ Pink

▨ Fuchsia

Rnd 13
Rnd 12
Rnd 11
Rnd 10
Rnd 9
Start of skirt

Rnd 8
Rnd 7
Row 6
Row 5
Row 4
Row 3
Row 2
Row 1
Yoke

SUPPLIES

· Bergère de France Coton Fifty yarn (#2 fine weight; 4 ply; 50% cotton, 50% acrylic; 153 yd/140 m per 1.8 oz/50 g) in Cytise (yellow) and Turquoise
· 3 mm (US C-2 or D-3) hook

FOR MARGUERITE

STITCHES AND TECHNIQUES

· Chain stitch, single crochet, single crochet increase or decrease: **see Stitches, page 34.**
· Fringe, Joining with whipstitch: **see Techniques, page 39.**

Notes: To change colors for the triangle, work stitches while laying non-working yarn on top of stitches being worked and crochet over them, or always carry the yellow yarn on the back side (jacquard/tapestry crochet).
Pm on the 1st sc of each rnd or row starting in Rnd 13.
Except when otherwise indicated, crochet with turquoise in Rows 1 through 7.

ROMPER OR ONE-PIECE SWIMSUIT

INSTRUCTIONS

The number between parentheses is the number of sts at the end of the row (or rnd).

Front

Note: Worked top down.

With turquoise, ch 18 sts.
Row 1: 1 sc in the 2nd ch from hook, 16 sc. (17 sts)
Row 2: Ch 1 to turn, 1 inc, 7 sc, ch 1 in yellow, 7 sc, 1 inc. (19 sts)
Row 3: Ch 1 to turn, 8 sc, 3 sc in yellow, 8 sc. (19 sts)
Row 4: Ch 1 to turn, 1 inc, 6 sc, 5 sc in yellow, 6 sc, 1 inc. (21 sts)
Row 5: Ch 1 to turn, 7 sc, 7 sc in yellow, 7 sc. (21 sts)
Row 6: Ch 1 to turn, 1 inc, 5 sc, 9 sc in yellow, 5 sc, 1 inc. (23 sts) Cut yellow yarn.
Row 7: Ch 1 to turn, 23 sc. (23 sts)
Row 8: With yellow, ch 1 to turn, 1 inc, 21 sc, 1 inc. (25 sts) Cut yellow yarn or work stitches over and encircle it in the next row. *(Note: Do same for following rows.)*
Row 9: With turquoise, ch 1 to turn, 25 sc. (25 sts) Cut turquoise yarn or work stitches over and encircle it in the next row. *(Note: Do same for following rows.)*
Row 10: With yellow, ch 1 to turn, 1 inc, 23 sc, 1 inc. (27 sts)
Row 11: With turquoise, ch 1 to turn, 27 sc. (27 sts)
Row 12: With yellow, ch 1 to turn, 1 inc, 25 sc, 1 inc. (29 sts) DO NOT CUT YELLOW YARN, leave it on hold on wrong side.
Rnd 13: With turquoise, ch 1 to turn, 29 sc, and then 29 ch sts for the back, join to work in round with sl st at the marker. (58 sts) DO NOT CUT TURQUOISE YARN, leave it on hold on wrong side.
Rnd 14: Pick up yellow yarn, ch 1, 1 inc, 13 sc, 1 inc, 13 sc, 1 inc, and then in the ch sts work 14 sc, 1 inc, 14 sc, sl st at the marker. (62 sts) Leave yellow yarn on hold.
Rnd 15: Pick up the turquoise yarn, ch 1, 62 sc, 1 sl st at the marker. (62 sts) Leave the turquoise yarn on hold on wrong side.
Rnd 16: Pick up yellow yarn, ch 1, 62 sc, sl st at the marker. (62 sts) Leave yellow yarn on hold on wrong side.
Rnd 17: Repeat Rnd 15.
Rnd 18: Repeat Rnd 16.
Then separate the work and continue in rows, alternating each color every 2 rows, starting with the turquoise (do not cut yarn, but carry them up the side; they will be hidden in the border).

Row 19: Ch 1, 31 sc, DO NOT WORK THE REMAINING STS. (31 sts)
Place a colored marker on the 1st remaining st.
Row 20: Ch 1 to turn, skip 1 st, sc2tog, 25 sc, sc2tog, DO NOT WORK THE LAST ST. (27 sts)
Row 21: Ch 1 to turn, skip 1 st, sc2tog, 21 sc, sc2tog, DO NOT WORK THE LAST ST. (23 sts)
Row 22: Ch 1 to turn, skip 1 st, sc2tog, 17 sc, sc2tog, DO NOT WORK THE LAST ST. (19 sts)
Row 23: Ch 1 to turn, sc2tog, 15 sc, sc2tog. (17 sts)
Row 24: Ch 1 to turn, skip 1 st, sc2tog, 11 sc, sc2tog, DO NOT WORK THE LAST ST. (13 sts)
Row 25: Ch 1 to turn, sc2tog, 9 sc, sc2tog. (11 sts)
Row 26: Ch 1 to turn, skip 1 st, sc2tog, 5 sc, sc2tog, DO NOT WORK THE LAST ST. (7 sts)
Row 27: Ch 1 to turn, sc2tog, 3 sc, sc2tog. (5 sts)
Row 28: Ch 1 to turn, sc2tog, 1 sc, sc2tog. (3 sts)
✓ Place colored marker on the 1st and last sts.
Rows 29-30: Ch 1 to turn, 3 sc. Cut yarn.

Back

Join turquoise yarn at marker from Rnd 18 and repeat Rows 19-30.
At the end of Row 30, leave yarn tail for sewing seam between legs.

Ruffles

Join yellow yarn to 1 st next to a marker, and then work 3 dc into the same st at the end of each row, working over and encircling the yarn carried up the edge, up to 2nd marker. Start again on the other side.

Straps

Join turquoise yarn to 1st st of foundation chain at top front, and then chain 30. Cut yarn.
Repeat on other side.
Tie in a knot behind doll's neck.

Fringe

Cut 9 strands of yarn approximately 5 in/12 cm long. Make fringe with 3 strands around the 13th sc on the front (= center st below triangle). Then make the other 2, placing them 4 sts apart on either side of the center one.
Even out bottom of fringe with scissors.

SUPPLIES

- Bergère de France Coton Fifty yarn (#2 fine weight; 4 ply; 50% cotton, 50% acrylic; 153 yd/140 m per 1.8 oz/50 g) in Berlingot (pink) and Coco (white)
- 2 small buttons
- 3 mm (US C-2 or D-3) hook

FOR DINA

STITCHES AND TECHNIQUES

- Magic circle, chain stitch, slip stitch, single crochet, double crochet invisible decrease, double crochet increase: **see Stitches, page 34.**
- **1 picot:** *ch 3, sl st in the front loop and the left vertical bar of the last sc*.

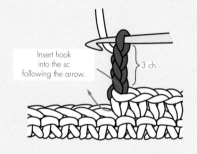

Insert hook into the sc following the arrow.

3 ch

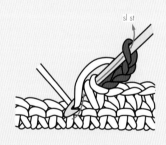

sl st

- Changing colors, joining with whipstitch: **see Techniques, page 39.**
- **Stripes:** Alternate 1 row in each color.

Note: Replace the 1st dc with ch 3 (pm in the 3rd ch).

SHORTALLS WITH POCKETS

INSTRUCTIONS

The number between parentheses is the number of sts at the end of the row (or rnd).

Top

With pink, ch 49 sts.

Row 1: 1 sc in the 2nd ch, 47 sc. (48 sts)

✓ Place colored marker in the 1st and last sts of the chain, in the loop not worked.

Rows 2-3: 48 dc. (48 sts)

Rnd 4: Repeat 4 times *11 dc, 1 inc*, and join in the round with sl st at the marker. (52 sts)

Rnd 5: Repeat 4 times *12 dc, 1 inc*, sl st at the marker. (56 sts)

Rnd 6: Repeat 8 times *6 dc, 1 inc*, sl st at the marker. (64 sts)

Rnd 7: 3 dc, 1 inc, repeat 7 times *7 dc, 1 inc*, 4 dc, sl st at the marker. (72 sts)

Rnds 8-9: 72 dc, sl st at the marker. (72 sts)

First Leg

Rnd 10: 36 dc, sl st at the marker. (36 sts) DO NOT WORK REMAINING STITCHES.

Rnd 11: 36 dc, sl st at the marker. (36 sts)

Rnd 12: Repeat 12 times *1 dc, 1 invisible dec*, sl st at the marker. (24 sts)

Rnds 13-14: 24 dc, sl st at the marker. (24 sts)

Rnd 15: Ch 1, 3 sc, repeat 7 times *1 picot, 3 sc*, sl st in the 1st sc, sl st in the 1st ch.

Cut yarn.

Second Leg

Join white yarn at the 1st st not worked in Rnd 9 and repeat Rnds 10-15.

Make 2 sts between legs to close.

Top Picot Edging

Join pink yarn on right side (legs toward the bottom) at a colored marker.

Rnd 1: Ch 1 (edge), repeat 15 times *3 sc, 1 picot*, 3 sc. *(Note: The last sc is at the second marker.)*

Cut yarn.

Straps

Reminder: The picots are separated by 3 sc. Join pink yarn on right side (legs toward the bottom) at the sc just after the 6th picot from the **back** opening (= start of front strap).

Row 1: 1 sc in the 2nd ch, 1 sc. (2 sts)

Rows 2-26: Ch 1 (edge), 2 sc. (2 sts)
Put the shortalls on the doll to check length of strap.
Attach with 2 sl st to the sc just after the 1st picot from
the **back** opening. Make sure not to twist the strap. Cut yarn.
Repeat for the second strap on the other side.
Sew 2 small buttons on the front at bottom of straps.

Pockets

Notes: Alternate 1 rnd pink and 1 rnd white.
The ch st at the beginning of the rnd does not replace the
1st sc (= turning ch).

With pink, start with a magic circle.
Rnd 1: Ch 1, 8 sc, sl st in the 1st sc, switch to the other
color when working the sl st. *(Note: Change colors each rnd.)*
Rnd 2: Ch 1, repeat 4 times *1 sc, [1 sc, ch 2, and 1 sc] in
the same st*, sl st in the 1st sc.
Rnd 3: Ch 1, 2 sc, [1 sc, ch 2, and 1 sc] in the ch-2 space
from previous rnd, repeat 3 times *3 sc, [1 sc, ch 2, and 1
sc] in the ch-2 space from the previous rnd*, 1 sc, sl st in
the 1st sc.
Rnd 4: Ch 1, 3 sc, [1 sc, ch 2, and 1 sc] in the ch-2 space
from the previous rnd, repeat 3 times *5 sc, [1 sc, ch 2,
and 1 sc] in the ch-2 space from the previous rnd*, 2 sc, sl
st in the 1st sc. Cut yarn, leaving a long tail for sewing.
Make a second identical pocket.

Thread the long tail onto the needle, inserting it from the
right side and bringing it up in a ch-2 space.
Sew pocket onto shortalls with whipstitch between rnds 7-10,
with a spacing of 5 dc (= pocket width). Don't work into all
sts, but make 1 st at each of the 4 corners and 3 others in
the middle of the sides. The spacing between the 2 pockets
is 22 dc on Rnd 7 (so 11 stitches out from the center). Tie
knot on reverse side.

BIKINI

INSTRUCTIONS

The number between parentheses is the number of sts at the
end of the rnd (or row).

Bottom

Top Band

Ch 54 sts and join to work in the round with sl st in the
1st ch.
Rnd 1: Ch 1, 1 sc (pm), 53 sc, sl st at the marker. (54 sts)
Rnd 2: Ch 1, 1 sc (pm), 53 sc, sl st in the front loop at the
marker. (54 sts)

SUPPLIES
· Bergère de France Coton
Fifty yarn (#2 fine weight;
4 ply; 50% cotton, 50%
acrylic; 153 yd/140 m per
1.8 oz/50 g) in Berlingot
(pink)
· 3.5 mm (US E-4) hook

FOR MARY-SUN

STITCHES AND TECHNIQUES

- Chain stitch, slip stitch, single crochet, single crochet 2 together: **see Stitches, page 34.**
- **Double decrease:** sc 3 together.
- Joining with whipstitch: **see Techniques, page 39.**

Note: The ch st at the beginning of the rnd or row is a turning ch; it does not replace the 1st sc.

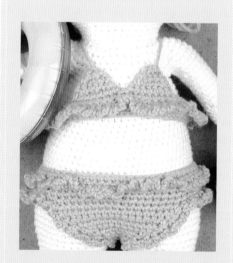

Rnd 3: *(Note: Work sc in the front loops and replace the marker in the same st, but only in the back unworked loop.)* Ch 1, 1 sc, repeat 53 times *ch 3, 1 sc*, sl st at the marker. (54 sts)

Rnd 4: *(Note: Only in the free back loop of sts from Rnd 2.)* Ch 1, 1 sc (pm), 53 sc, sl st at the marker. (54 sts)

Rnds 5-7: Ch 1, 1 sc (pm), 53 sc, sl st at the marker. Then separate the work and work in rows.

Front

Row 8: Ch 1, 18 sc. (18 sts) DO NOT WORK OTHER STS.

Row 9: Ch 1 to turn, sc2tog, 14 sc, sc2tog. (16 sts)

Row 10: Ch 1 to turn, sc2tog, 12 sc, sc2tog. (14 sts)

Row 11: Ch 1 to turn, sc2tog, 10 sc, sc2tog. (12 sts)

Row 12: Ch 1 to turn, 1 double dec (sc3tog), 6 sc, 1 double dec. (8 sts)

Row 13: Ch 1 to turn, sc2tog, 4 sc, sc2tog. (6 sts)

Row 14: Ch 1 to turn, sc2tog, 2 sc, sc2tog. (4 sts)

Row 15: Ch 1 to turn, 2 sc2tog. (2 sts)

Row 16: Ch 1 to turn, 2 sc. Cut yarn.

Back

Skip 9 sts, join yarn and repeat Rnds 8-16.
Whipstitch the 2 center sts together.

Leg Edging

Join yarn at one of the 9 sts not worked, ch 1, repeat all the way around *1 sc, ch 3*, sl st in the 1st sc, ch 1 to close and cut yarn.
Repeat on the other side.

Top

Ch 52 sts, leaving 6 in/15 cm of yarn at the beginning.

Row 1: 1 sc in the 2nd ch from hook, 50 sc. (51 sts)

Row 2: Ch 1 to turn, 51 sc. (51 sts)

Row 3: *(Note: Only in the front loop of the sts.)* Ch 1 to turn, 1 sc, repeat 51 times *ch 3, 1 sc*.

Row 4: *(Note: Only in the back loop of Row 2 sts.)* Ch 1 to turn, 51 sc. (51 sts)

Row 5: Ch 1 to turn, 51 sc. (51 sts) Cut yarn. Skip 18 sts, join yarn at the 19th sc of Row 5.

Row 6: Ch 1 (edge), 7 sc. (7 sts)

Row 7: Ch 1 to turn, sc2tog, 3 sc, sc2tog. (5 sts)

Row 8: Ch 1 to turn, sc2tog, 1 sc, sc2tog. (3 sts)

Row 9: Ch 1 to turn, 1 double dec (sc3tog). Cut enough yarn for the strap.

Skip 1 st, join yarn to the 27th sc of Row 5, and then repeat Rows 6-9.

Tie straps around neck.

SHOES

BOOTIES IN FIVE VERSIONS:
WITH POM-POMS, FRINGE, LACES, RIBS, and CUFFS

INSTRUCTIONS

The number between parentheses is the number of sts at the end of the rnd.

Basic Pattern for Versions with Pom-Poms, Fringe, Laces, and Cuffs

Note: Work increases in sc.

Start with a magic circle.
Rnd 1: Ch 1, 1 sc (pm), 5 sc. (6 sts)
Rnd 2: 6 inc. (12 sts)
Rnd 3: Repeat 6 times *1 sc, 1 inc*, sl st in the back loop at the marker. (18 sts)
Rnd 4: *(Note: In the back loop only of the stitches from previous rnd.)* Ch 3 (pm in the 3rd ch), 1 dc, dc2tog, repeat 3 times *2 dc, dc2tog*, 2 dc, sl st at the marker. (14 sts)
Rnds 5-8: Ch 3 (= 1st dc, pm in the 3rd ch), 13 dc, 1 sl st at the marker. (14 sts)
Cut yarn (except for version with cuff).
Make another identical basic version.

SUPPLIES
- Bergère de France Idéal (#3 light weight; 30% acrylic, 30% polyamide, 40% combed wool; 136 yd/124 m per 1.8 oz/50 g) or Bergère de France Coton Fifty (#2 fine weight; 4 ply; 50% cotton, 50% acrylic; 153 yd/140 m per 1.8 oz/50 g) yarn in your choice of color
- 3.5 mm (US E-4) hook

FOR VIOLET   FOR PIA   FOR DOMI

FOR FAWNTINE   FOR ANNA   FOR PIKI

FOR TINA   FOR JOSETTE   FOR AVERY

FOR EMORY

STITCHES AND TECHNIQUES
- Magic circle, chain stitch, slip stitch, single crochet, single and double crochet increases, double crochet 2 together, front post double crochet: **see Stitches, page 34.**
- Working in a spiral, fringe: **see Techniques, page 39.**

Note: Rnds 1-3: Work in a spiral in sc, pm in the 1st sc at the start of each rnd.

CLOTHING & ACCESSORIES

Pom-Pom Booties

Note: Make increases in sc.

Start with a magic circle, leaving a yarn tail of about 4 in/10 cm at the beginning.
Rnd 1: Ch 1, 1 sc (pm), 5 sc. (6 sts)
Rnd 2: 6 inc. (12 sts)
Ch 1 to fasten off and cut yarn, also leaving 4 in/10 cm on this end.
Thread this yarn onto the needle and insert it in the 12 sts (into the right side, then into the wrong side, etc.), and then pull yarn to tighten and form a small ball.
Attach the pom-pom around 1 dc from the last rnd, sliding the yarn ends around each side of the dc, and then make 2 knots on the reverse side of the work. Repeat these same steps for the other bootie.

Fringed Booties

Note: Start by weaving in the 2 yarn ends from the bootie.
Cut 14 strands of beige yarn about 3 in/8 cm long and attach fringe inserting the hook in the sts in the next-to-the-last rnd.

Thread a long strand of yarn on the needle, insert it into the back side of a st through the 2 loops. Take it over the knot formed by the fringe (tighten the fringe knot by pulling down on the 2 strands) and reinsert under the same st. Repeat for fringe in the next 13 sts.
This "traps" the knot so it won't easily become undone. This also helps keep the fringe directed toward the bottom.
Even ends of fringe with scissors.
Repeat these same steps for the other bootie.

Laced Booties

Thread contrasting yarn onto the needle; then insert from the wrong side toward the front between 2 dc from Rnd 4 (**see 1 on the diagram**), leaving a long tail (this will be used later), and then skip over 1 st in the same rnd and insert the needle (2), bring it up diagonally in the top of the same st from Rnd 4 (3), above (1), and insert the needle at (4). Continue following this same pattern until the last rnd (10).
Take the beginning tail of yarn (in blue on diagram) and do the same steps on the opposite side. Keep in place with 2 knots on the reverse side before weaving in ends. Repeat these same steps for the other bootie.

Booties with Cuff

Note: Make increases in dc.

Continue on from basic pattern as follows:
Rnd 9: (IN FRONT LOOPS ONLY): [Ch 3 (= 1st dc, pm in the 3rd ch) and 1 dc] in the same st, 13 inc, sl st at the marker, changing colors in sl st. (28 sts)
Rnd 10: Ch 1 to turn, 28 sc. (28 sts)
Cut yarn.
Fold over top to make cuff such that the stitches not worked in Rnd 8 are visible on the top.
Make another identical bootie.

Ribbed Booties

Start with a magic circle.
Rnd 1: Ch 1, 1 sc (pm), 5 sc. (6 sts)
Rnd 2: 6 inc. (12 sts)
Rnd 3: Repeat 6 times *1 sc, 1 inc*, sl st at the marker in the back loop. (18 sts)
Rnd 4: (Only in the BACK LOOP of the sts from previous rnd), ch 3 (pm in the 3rd ch), 1 dc, dc2tog, repeat 3 times *2 dc, dc2tog*, 2 dc, sl st at the marker. (14 sts)
Rnds 5-8: Ch 3 (= 1st dc, pm in the 3rd ch), repeat 6 times *1 front post dc, 1 dc*, 1 front post dc, sl st at the marker. (14 sts)

Note: For front post dc on the decreases, insert around the 2 dc of the dec.

Cut yarn.
Make another identical bootie.

Lacing Pattern

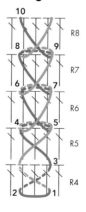

BUNNY SLIPPERS

INSTRUCTIONS

The number between parentheses is the number of sts at the end of the rnd (or row).

Slippers
Start with a magic circle.
Rnd 1: Ch 1, 6 sc. (6 sts)
Rnd 2: 6 inc. (12 sts)
Rnd 3: Repeat 6 times *1 sc, 1 inc*. (18 sts)
Rnd 4: Repeat 6 times *2 sc, 1 inc*. (24 sts)
Rnd 5: 24 sc in back loop only. (24 sts)
Rnd 6: Repeat 6 times *2 sc, sc2tog*. (18 sts)
Rnds 7-8: 18 sc. (18 sts) Then separate the work.
Rnd 9: First ear, 2 sc, DO NOT WORK REMAINING STS. (2 sts)
Rnds 10-12: Ch 1 to turn, 2 sc. (2 sts)
Rnd 13: Ch 1 to turn, sc2tog.
Cut yarn.
Skip 1 st from Rnd 8 after the first ear, join yarn and repeat Rnds 9-13 for the **second ear**.
Make another identical slipper.

Bunny Head
Start with a magic circle.
Rnd 1: Ch 1, 5 sc. (5 sts)
Rnd 2: 5 inc. (10 sts)
Rnd 3: Repeat 5 times *1 sc, 1 inc*. (15 sts)
Rnd 4: Repeat 5 times *1 sc, sc2tog*. (10 sts) Cut yarn, leaving a long tail for sewing.
Sew head to slipper with whipstitch, centering it between ears. No need to stuff it. Push on it to flatten a bit. Make another identical head.

Face
Sew 1 bead on each side of the head on Rnd 3 for the eyes (see photo).
Sew 1 bead in the center (the hole of the magic circle) for the nose, and then embroider the mouth with 2 straight stitches over Rnd 1. Make identical face on the other slipper.

STRIPED SOCKS

INSTRUCTIONS

The number between parentheses is the number of sts at the end of the rnd.
With black, start with a magic circle.
Rnd 1: Ch 1, 6 sc. (6 sts)
Rnd 2: 6 inc. (12 sts)

SUPPLIES
- Bergère de France Coton Fifty yarn (#2 fine weight; 4 ply; 50% cotton, 50% acrylic; 153 yd/140 m per 1.8 oz/50 g) in Berlingot (pink) or Glycine (violet), a bit of Zan (black)
- 6 small black beads
- 3 mm (US C-2 or D-3) hook

FOR DINA

FOR SOPHIA

STITCHES AND TECHNIQUES
- Magic circle, chain stitch, single crochet, working in the back loop only, single crochet increase or decrease (sc2tog): **see Stitches, page 34.**
- Working in a spiral, joining with whipstitch: **see Techniques, page 39.**
- Straight stitch: **see Embroidery Stitches, page 38.**

Notes: For rnds (to be worked in spiral), pm in the 1st sc of each rnd.
Crochet entire slipper in pink (or violet).

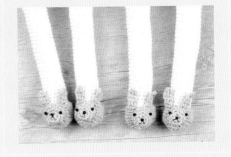

SUPPLIES
- Bergère de France Coton Fifty yarn (#2 fine weight; 4 ply; 50% cotton, 50% acrylic; 153 yd/140 m per 1.8 oz/50 g) in Zan (black) and Berlingot (pink)
- 3 mm (US C-2 or D-3) hook

FOR NINA

115

STITCHES AND TECHNIQUES

· Magic circle, chain stitch, slip stitch, single crochet, working in the back loop only, single crochet increase: **see Stitches, page 34.**

· Working in a spiral, changing colors: **see Techniques, page 39.**

Note: Pm in the 1st sc of each rnd.

SUPPLIES

· Bergère de France Coton Fifty yarn (#2 fine weight; 4 ply; 50% cotton, 50% acrylic; 153 yd/140 m per 1.8 oz/50 g) in the following colors: Berlingot (pink), a bit of Coco (white); or Turquoise, a bit of Zan (black); or Ecarlate (red), a bit of Zan (black)

· 3 mm (US C-2 or D-3) hook

FOR MARGUERITE FOR ROSIE FOR ABBOTT

STITCHES AND TECHNIQUES

· Magic circle, chain stitch, single crochet, single crochet increase, sc2tog or dc2tog: **see Stitches, page 34.**

· Working in a spiral: **see Techniques, page 39.**

Rnd 3: Repeat 6 times *1 sc, 1 inc*. (18 sts)

Rnd 4: Repeat 6 times *2 sc, 1 inc*. (24 sts)

Rnd 5: 24 sc in back loop only. (24 sts)

Rnd 6: Repeat 6 times *2 sc, sc2tog*. (18 sts) Change colors in the last st of the rnd, BUT DO NOT CUT YARN.

Rnds 7-13: 18 sc, changing colors in the last st of each rnd (DO NOT CUT YARN).

Rnd 14: With pink, sl st at the marker, sl st in the next st, repeat 4 times *skip 1 st, 4 sc in the following st, skip 1 st, 1 sl st*, 1 sl st.

Cut yarn (= back side of sock).

Make another identical sock.

SHOES WITH BOW

INSTRUCTIONS

The number between parentheses is the number of sts at the end of the rnd (or row).

Start with a magic circle.

Rnd 1: Ch 1, 1 sc (pm), 6 sc. (7 sts)

Rnd 2: [1 sc (pm) and 1 sc] in the same st, 6 inc. (14 sts)

Rnd 3: 1 sc (pm), 1 inc, repeat 6 times *1 sc, 1 inc*. (21 sts)

Rnd 4: Work into back loop only, 1 sc (pm), 3 sc, sc2tog, repeat 2 times *4 sc, sc2tog*, 3 sc. (18 sts)

Rnd 5: 1 sc (pm around the sc for the tie), ch 1, skip 1 st, repeat 8 times *1 sc, ch 1, skip 1 st*. (18 sts)

Rnd 6: 1 sc (pm), 17 sc, sl st at the marker. (18 sts)

Rnd 7: Ch 2, 1 dc (pm), 14 dc, dc2tog. (16 sts) DO NOT JOIN IN THE ROUND.

Rnd 8: Ch 1 to turn, 16 sc. (16 sts)

Cut yarn.

For the tie, insert needle with contrasting color yarn under the center st, and then bring needle once behind the sc marker, once in front of the next sc in Rnd 5, continuing around until you come back to the beginning. Put shoe on doll, tie 2 knots and make a little bow.

Make another identical shoe.

BALLET FLATS

INSTRUCTIONS

The number between parentheses is the number of sts at the end of the rnd.

Start with a magic circle.

Rnd 1: Ch 1, 1 sc (pm), 5 sc. (6 sts)

Rnd 2: 6 inc. (12 sts)

Rnd 3: Repeat 6 times *1 sc, 1 inc*, join to work in the round with 1 sl st at the marker. (18 sts)

Rnd 4: Ch 3 (pm in the 3rd ch), 13 dc, ch 3, skip remaining 5 sts, sl st at the marker.

Rnd 5: Ch 3 (pm in the 3rd ch), dc2tog, 8 dc, dc2tog, 1 dc, 3 sc in the ch space, sl st at the marker.

Rnd 6: Ch 1 (pm = 1st sl st), 11 sl st, DO NOT WORK THE REMAINING STS.

Cut yarn.

Make another identical ballet flat.

FAIRY SHOES

INSTRUCTIONS

Shoes

The number between parentheses is the number of sts at the end of the rnd (or row).

Start with a magic circle.

Rnd 1: 5 dc, join to work in the round with sl st at the marker. (5 sts)

Rnd 2: 5 inc, sl st at the marker. (10 sts)

Rnd 3: Repeat 5 times *1 dc, 1 inc*, sl st at the marker. (15 sts)

Row 4: 1 inc, 2 dc, 1 inc, 5 dc, 1 inc, 2 dc, 1 inc, 2 dc. (19 sts) *Note: For remainder of pattern, do not join in the round.*

Row 5: Turn, 8 dc, dc3tog, 8 dc. (17 sts)

Row 6: Turn, 2 dc, 1 hdc, 2 sc, sc2tog, sc3tog, sc2tog, 2 sc, 1 hdc, 2 dc. (13 sts)

Cut yarn, leaving a long tail to sew back seam.

SUPPLIES

· Bergère de France Idéal yarn (#3 light weight; 30% acrylic, 30% polyamide, 40% combed wool; 136 yd/124 m per 1.8 oz/50 g) in Beige Rose (dusty rose) or Sequoia (mahogany); or Bergère de France Coton Fifty yarn (#2 fine weight; 4 ply; 50% cotton, 50% acrylic; 153 yd/140 m per 1.8 oz/50 g) in Nectarine (coral)

· 3.5 mm (US E-4) hook

FOR AGATHA   FOR JO   FOR GRETA

FOR HYACINTH & ROSEMARY

STITCHES AND TECHNIQUES

· Magic circle, chain stitch, slip stitch, single crochet, single crochet increase, double crochet, double crochet 2 together: **see Stitches, page 34.**

· Working in a spiral: **see Techniques, page 39.**

Note: Work in a spiral for the first two rnds, and pm in the 1st st.

SUPPLIES

· Bergère de France Coton Fifty yarn (#2 fine weight; 4 ply; 50% cotton, 50% acrylic; 153 yd/140 m per 1.8 oz/50 g) in the following colors: Gingembre (orange), Bengale (fuchsia), Berlingot (pink), Turquoise, Cytise (yellow)

· 3 mm (US C-2 or D-3) hook

FOR SALOME

FOR LOLY

117

STITCHES AND TECHNIQUES

· Magic circle, chain stitch, half double crochet, double crochet, double crochet increase, single crochet 2 together: **see Stitches, page 34.**
· **Dc 5 together:** Repeat 5 times in the same st *yo, insert hook in the st, yo and pull through the st, yo, pull through 2 loops*, yo and pull through all 6 loops on the hook.
· Joining with whipstitch: **see Techniques, page 39.**

Notes: Replace the 1st dc with ch 3 and pm in the 3rd ch (not indicated in the instructions). For 2-color versions: Alternate 1 rnd/row in fuchsia (or pink) and 1 rnd/row in yellow (or turquoise).

TIP

Replace the crocheted pom-pom with a small light felt one and sew it with matching thread.

SUPPLIES

· Your choice of yarn
· Hook appropriate for selected yarn

STITCHES AND TECHNIQUES

· **Foundation double crochet:** Ch 2, *yo, insert hook into the 2nd ch from hook, yo and pull through st, yo and pull through 1 loop only on the hook (place marker in this chain just made until you get used to the technique), yo and pull through 1 loop on hook, repeat 2 times °°yo and pull through 2 loops on hook°°*, repeat from * to * the number of sts indicated, inserting hook into the ch st at the base of the dc just made (st with marker).

Use whipstitch to sew up the back of the shoe over 5 sts.
Make another identical shoe.

Pom-Poms

Start with a ch 2, leaving a tail of yarn at the beginning for sewing.
Row 1: [Dc5tog and 1 sl st] in the 1st ch.
Cut yarn, leaving a tail for sewing.
Pull on the 2 yarn tails to form a nice round ball.
Make a second identical pom-pom.

FINISHING

Attach a small pom-pom to the point (toe) of the shoe, sliding 1 yarn end through each side of the magic circle and knotting them twice on the reverse side.

– ACCESSORIES –

QUICK SCARF

INSTRUCTIONS

Work a foundation double crochet for the desired length. And that's it! It's done!

SCALLOPED COLLAR

INSTRUCTIONS

The number between parentheses is the number of sts at the end of the row.

With turquoise (or coral), ch 38 sts, leaving a long enough tail for the **first tie**.

Row 1: 1 sc (pm) in the 2nd ch from hook, 36 sc. (37 sts)

Row 2: Turn, ch 1 (= 1st sl st, pm), skip the first 2 sc, repeat 8 times *5 dc in the same st, skip 1 st, 1 sl st, skip 1 st*, 5 dc in the same st, skip 1 st, sl st at the marker. (55 sts) Cut yarn.

Row 3: Join fuchsia (or yellow) yarn at the marker, ch 1 (edge), 1 sc in the marker, repeat 8 times *5 sc in the 5 dc from Row 2, 1 extended sl st in the base of the sl st from Row 2 (= as to make 1 sl st in the same st as in Row 2)*, 5 sc in the 5 dc from Row 2, 1 sl st. (55 sts) Cut yarn.

Join a strand of turquoise (or coral) yarn on the other side of Row 1 for the **second tie**.

Tie around the neck.

TULLE OR LACE RUFF

INSTRUCTIONS

With Yarn

Make 1 triple knot (to block the tulle) at 6 in/15 cm from one end of the yarn (for the tie), and then thread onto the needle. Insert needle in the center of the tulle (or lace) and baste along the entire length in running stitch, spacing out the stitches by about 0.4 in/1 cm.

Little by little, gather the strip of tulle/lace along the running stitches from one end to the other.

Then position it on the doll's neck and pull the yarn up to the knot. Mark this spot with felt-tip pen. Remove from doll and make 1 triple knot where marked.

Leave 6 in/15 cm tail of yarn and cut.

Place collar around the neck and tie with the 2 yarn tails, making a bow.

With Elastic Cord

Thread the elastic cord onto the needle, and in the center of the tulle/lace, baste along the entire length in running stitch, spacing out the stitches by about 0.4 in/1 cm.

Little by little, gather the strip of tulle/lace along the running stitches from one end to the other.

Then position it on the doll's neck and tie 2 knots to secure (without pulling on the elastic). The collar can then be put on the doll by stretching the elastic.

SUPPLIES
· Bergère de France Coton Fifty yarn (#2 fine weight; 4 ply; 50% cotton, 50% acrylic; 153 yd/140 m per 1.8 oz/50 g) in Turquoise, Bengale (fuchsia) or Nectarine (coral), Cytise (yellow)
· 3 mm (C-2 or D-3) hook

FOR PIKI

STITCHES AND TECHNIQUES
· Chain stitch, slip stitch, single crochet, double crochet: **see Stitches, page 34.**

SUPPLIES
· 3 × 43 in/8 × 110 cm piece of tulle or lace
· A bit of Coton Fifty (or Idéal) yarn OR fine elastic cord
· Felt-tip pen

FOR ROSIE

119

SUPPLIES

· Bergère de France Coton Fifty yarn (#2 fine weight; 4 ply; 50% cotton, 50% acrylic; 153 yd/140 m per 1.8 oz/50 g) in Coquille (peach beige)
· 3 mm (C-2 or D-3) hook

FOR SALOMÉ

STITCHES AND TECHNIQUES

· Chain stitch, slip stitch, single crochet, triple crochet: **see Stitches, page 34.**
· Working around a chain: **see Techniques, page 39.**

Note: Replace the 1st triple crochet with ch 4 (pm in the 4th ch).

SUPPLIES

· Bergère de France Coton Fifty yarn (#2 fine weight; 4 ply; 50% cotton, 50% acrylic; 153 yd/140 m per 1.8 oz/50 g) in Turquoise
· 1 decorative heart-shaped button
· 3.5 mm (US E-4) hook

FOR JOSETTE

STITCHES AND TECHNIQUES

· Chain stitch, slip stitch, single crochet, double crochet, single crochet increase, double crochet 2 together: **see Stitches, page 34.**
· Working around a chain, working in spiral: **see Techniques, page 39.**

Notes: Work Rnds 1–4 in a spiral. Pm on the 1st st of each rnd (and starting in Rnd 6, in the 3rd ch of the 1st dc).

SHOULDER BAG
INSTRUCTIONS

See bag in the photo on page 14.
The number between parentheses indicates the number of sts at the end of the rnd.
Chain 11.
Rnd 1: 1 sc in the 2nd chain from hook (pm), 9 sc, move to other side of the chain, 10 sc, sl st at the marker. (20 sts)
Rnds 2–4: 20 triple crochet.
Rnd 5: Ch 62, skip 9 sts and close with a sl st to form the strap.
Cut yarn.

BACKPACK
INSTRUCTIONS

The number between parentheses indicates the number of sts at the end of the rnd (or row).

Bag
Chain 7.
Rnd 1: 1 sc in the 2nd ch from hook, 5 sc, move to other side of the chain, 6 sc. (12 sts)
Rnd 2: 1 inc, 4 sc, 2 inc, 4 sc, 1 inc. (16 sts)
Rnd 3: 1 sc, 1 inc, 4 sc, 1 inc, 2 sc, 1 inc, 4 sc, 1 inc, 1 sc. (20 sts)
Rnd 4: 2 sc, 1 inc, 4 sc, 1 inc, 4 sc, 1 inc, 4 sc, 1 inc, 2 sc. (24 sts)
Rnd 5: 3 sc, 1 inc, 4 sc, 1 inc, 6 sc, 1 inc, 4 sc, 1 inc, 3 sc, sl st in the 1st sc. (28 sts)
Rnd 6: Ch 3 (= 1st dc), 27 dc, sl st at the marker. (28 sts)
✓ Place a colored marker around the 5th dc and the 13th dc.
Rnds 7–9: Ch 3 (= 1st dc), 27 dc, sl st at the marker. (28 sts) DO NOT CUT YARN.

Flap
Row 10: 4 sl st, ch 3 (= 1st dc), 9 dc. (10 sts) DO NOT WORK REMAINING STS.
Row 11: [Ch 2, 1 dc] (= dec, pm in the dc), 6 dc, dc2tog. (8 sts)
Row 12: [Ch 2, 1 dc] (= dec, pm in the dc), 4 dc, dc2tog. (6 sts)
Row 13: Ch 3 (= 1st dc), 5 dc. (6 sts)
Cut yarn.

Straps
Skip 1 st after the beginning of the flap and join yarn.
Row 1: Ch 20 and join to work in the round with sl st around the dc with colored marker on back of bag.
Row 2: Ch 1, 24 sc in the ch, sl st in the 1st st at beginning. Cut yarn.
Make another identical strap.
Sew button to front of bag and slip it between 2 dc on flap to button.

FRINGED BAG

INSTRUCTIONS

The number between parentheses is the number of sts at the end of the rnd (or row).

Bag
With black yarn and mercerized cotton held together (for marled effect), ch 11 sts.
Row 1: 1 dc in the 5th ch from hook, 6 dc. (8 sts)
Rows 2-8: Turn, 8 dc. (8 sts)
✓ Place colored marker in the 1st and last dc of Row 6.
Cut yarn.

White Point
Join white Coton Fifty to the last dc, and then:
Row 1: Ch 1 (edge), 1 sc, 1 hdc, 1 dc, 2 tr, 1 dc, 1 hdc, 1 sc.
Cut yarn.

FINISHING

Fringe
Cut 7 strands of mercerized cotton approximately 4⅓ in/11 cm long (or 5 strands of white Coton Fifty), and use them to make a fringe at the point, between the 2 tr.
Fold the flap at markers and sew sides together with whipstitch.

Strap
Join black yarn to a seam st (on the last row), ch 40 (or more for a longer strap), 1 sl st on the other side.
Cut yarn.
Sew half of snap to the wrong side of a tr in the white point and the other half to matching spot on Row 2 of the bag.

SATCHEL

INSTRUCTIONS

The number between parentheses is the number of sts at the end of the row.

Sides and Bottom of Satchel
With fuchsia, ch 27 (leaving long yarn tail at beginning for sewing).
Row 1: 1 sc in the 2nd ch from hook, 25 sc. (26 sts)
Cut yarn.

SUPPLIES
· Bergère de France Coton Fifty yarn (#2 fine weight; 4 ply; 50% cotton, 50% acrylic; 153 yd/140 m per 1.8 oz/50 g) in Zan (black) and Coco (white)
· Mercerized cotton (100% Egyptian cotton; 617 yd/565 m per 3.5 oz/100 g) in white (optional)
· 1 small snap
· 3.5 mm (US E-4) hook

FOR NINA

STITCHES AND TECHNIQUES
· Chain stitch, single crochet, half double crochet, double crochet, triple crochet: **see Stitches, page 34.**
· Fringe, joining with whipstitch: **see Techniques, page 39.**

Note: Starting in Row 2, replace the 1st dc with ch 3.

SUPPLIES
· Bergère de France Coton Fifty yarn (#2 fine weight; 4 ply; 50% cotton, 50% acrylic; 153 yd/140 m per 1.8 oz/50 g) in Bengale (fuchsia), a bit of Zan (black)
· 1 snap
· 3 mm (US C-2 or D-3) hook

FOR MARY-SUN

STITCHES AND TECHNIQUES

· Chain stitch, slip stitch, single crochet, double crochet: see **Stitches, page 34.**
· Joining with whipstitch: see **Techniques, page 39.**

Note: Replace the 1st dc in the row with ch 3 (pm in the 3rd ch).

SUPPLIES

· Bergère de France Coton Fifty yarn (#2 fine weight; 4 ply; 50% cotton, 50% acrylic; 153 yd/140 m per 1.8 oz/50 g) in the following colors: Turquoise, Berlingot (pink), Cytise (yellow), Coquille (peach-beige), Bengale (fuchsia)
· 1 medium snap
· 2.5 mm (US B-1 or C-2) and 3.5 mm (US E-4) hooks

FOR TINA

Back and Flap

Row 2: Skip 8 sts, join fuchsia yarn, 10 dc. (10 sts)
Rows 3-5: Turn, 10 dc. (10 sts)
✓ Place colored marker around the 4th and 7th dc of Row 4.
Row 6: Ch 1, turn, 10 sc. (10 sts) Cut yarn.

Edging on Flap

With black, join yarn to the side of the 1st dc of Row 5 and work 2 sl st in 1 loop, 1 sl st on the side of the last sc of Row 6, 1 ch (= corner), 10 sl st, 1 ch (= corner), and again 1 sc on the side of the last sc of Row 6, 2 sl st around 1 loop of the dc.
Cut yarn.

Front

Join the fuchsia yarn on the other side of Row 1 at 8 sts from the edge (so opposite the back).
Rows 2-3: 10 dc. (10 sts)
Row 4: Ch 1, turn, 10 sc. (10 sts) Cut yarn, leaving a tail for sewing.

FINISHING

With whipstitch, sew together the ends of the rows from the back and front to the 8 sts from Row 1, slide the yarn under the small band and continue on the other side, joining in the same way.

Handle

Row 1: Join fuchsia yarn at marker, ch 6, sl st around 2nd marker.
Row 2: Ch 1, 10 sc in the ch-5 space, 1 sl st in the space. Cut yarn.

Sew one side of snap to the center of the flap and the other side directly opposite it on the front.

FLOWER CROWN

INSTRUCTIONS

The number between parentheses indicates the number of sts at the end of the row.

Base Band

With turquoise, ch 57 sts (pm in the last ch).
Row 1: 1 dc in the 5th ch, 52 dc. (54 sts)
Row 2: Ch 3 (= 1st dc, pm in the 3rd ch), turn, 53 dc. (54 sts) Cut yarn.

Place band on doll's head as in photo on page 123. At back of head, pm on the 2 sts that overlap. Sew snap to these ends.

Embellishments

Note: Prepare the various embellishments (flowers and leaves), leaving a long yarn tail at the beginning and end of each one to sew them onto the band.

Large Leaves

With turquoise, ch 8 sts (pm in the last ch st).
Row 1: Sl st in the 2nd ch from hook, 1 sc, 1 hdc, 1 dc, 1 hdc, 1 sc, 1 sl st, ch 1, move to other side of the chain, 1 sc, 1 hdc, 1 dc, 1 hdc, 1 sc, 1 sl st, join in the round with sl st at the marker (= point of leaf).
Cut yarn and weave in this last end along the length of the leaf, bringing it out a few sts before the start of the chain.
Make 6 other identical leaves.

Small Leaves

With turquoise, ch 7 sts (pm in the last ch).
Row 1: Sl st in the 2nd ch from hook, 1 sc, 2 hdc, 1 sc, 1 sl st.
Cut.
Make 3 other identical small leaves.

Large Flowers

With yellow, start with a magic circle.
Rnd 1: Ch 1, 1 sc (pm), 4 sc (= 5 sts), sl st at the marker, switching to pink (or fuchsia or peach-beige).
Rnd 2: Ch 5 (pm in the 1st ch), 1 tr, ch 4, repeat 4 times *[1 sl st, ch 4, and 1 tr] in the next st, ch 4*, sl st at the marker. Cut yarn.
In all, make 2 large flowers in yellow/pink, 2 in yellow/fuchsia, and 1 in yellow/peach-beige.

Small Flowers

Start with a magic circle.
Rnd 1: Repeat 5 times *ch 2, dc2tog, ch 2, 1 sl st*, 1 sl st.
In all, make 3 small flowers in peach-beige, 2 in pink, 2 in yellow, and 1 in fuchsia.

FINISHING

Slip stitch the different elements onto the band.

Correctly Block All Pieces

Wet the band and lay it flat on a towel, spreading out the petals and leaves, and then fold the towel over the top. Press down firmly (by walking on it, for example, it's very effective), unfold the towel and let dry.

STITCHES AND TECHNIQUES

· Magic circle, chain stitch, single crochet, half double crochet, double crochet, triple crochet: **see Stitches, page 34.**
· Changing colors, working around a chain: **see Techniques, page 39.**
· Foundation double crochet: **see Quick Scarf, page 118.**

TIP

To have ties on the back, attach a foundation double chain of the desired length at either end of the band (see Quick Scarf page 118).

SUPPLIES

• Bergère de France Coton Fifty yarn (#2 fine weight; 4 ply; 50% cotton, 50% acrylic; 153 yd/140 m per 1.8 oz/50 g) in Perle (gray) and Glycine (violet)
• 3 mm (US C-2 or D-3) hook

STITCHES AND TECHNIQUES

Magic circle, chain stitch, slip stitch, single crochet, double crochet, triple crochet: **see Stitches, page 34.**

HEADBAND WITH BOW

INSTRUCTIONS

The number between parentheses indicates the number of sts at the end of the row (or rnd).

Headband

With gray, ch 60 sts (pm in the last ch).
Row 1: 1 dc in the 5th ch, 55 dc. (57 sts) Cut yarn.
Row 2: With violet, ch 25 sts (= tie), and then attach to work with 1 sc at the marker (pm), 56 sc, then again ch 25 sts (= tie). Cut yarn.
Row 3: Join gray yarn at marker, ch 1 (edge), repeat 14 times *1 sc, skip 1 st, 5 dc in the next st, skip 1 st*, finish with 1 sc. Cut yarn.

FINISHING

Bow

With gray, start with a magic circle.
Row 1: Repeat 2 times *ch 4, 4 tr, ch 4, 1 sl st in the circle*.
Cut yarn.
Leave a long length of violet yarn, wrap it around the center and tie knot on back. Sew the bow to the center of the headband.

Use ties to secure headband to doll's head.

HAIR BOW

INSTRUCTIONS

The number between parentheses is the number of sts at the end of the row.
Start with a magic circle, leaving 8 in/20 cm of yarn tail at the beginning.
Row 1: Repeat 2 times *ch 3, 3 dc, ch 3 in the circle*.

For a smaller bow (like the white one on the braid in photo):
Row 1: Repeat 2 times *ch 3, 2 dc, ch 3, 1 sl st in the circle*.

Cut yarn, leaving a tail about 8 in/20 cm long.
Make another identical bow.
Wrap the last yarn tail around the center of the bow 4 times, and then make 2 tight knots on the back with the yarn tail from the beginning.
Using the 2 lengths of yarn, attach the bow to a pigtail, bun, or the bottom of a braid.

TRIANGLE THROW BLANKET

INSTRUCTIONS

The number between parentheses is the number of sts at the end of the rnd (or row).
With turquoise, chain 34 sts, place marker on the last ch.
Row 1: 1 dc in the 5th ch, 5 dc, 1 fuchsia dc, repeat 2 times *7 turquoise dc, 1 fuchsia dc*, 7 turquoise dc. (31 sts)
Row 2: Ch 2 to turn, 1 fuchsia dc, repeat 3 times *5 turquoise dc, 3 fuchsia dc*, 5 turquoise dc, 1 fuchsia dc.
Row 3: Ch 2 to turn, 2 fuchsia dc, repeat 3 times *3 turquoise dc, 5 fuchsia dc*, 3 turquoise dc, 2 fuchsia dc.
Row 4: Ch 2 to turn, 3 fuchsia dc, repeat 3 times *1 turquoise dc, 7 fuchsia dc*, 1 turquoise dc, 3 fuchsia dc.
Row 5: Ch 2 to turn, 3 yellow dc, 1 white dc, repeat 3 times *7 yellow dc, 1 white dc*, 3 yellow dc.
Row 6: Ch 2 to turn, 2 yellow dc, 3 white dc, repeat 3 times *5 yellow dc, 3 white dc*, 2 yellow dc.
Row 7: Ch 2 to turn, 1 yellow dc, 5 white dc, repeat 3 times *3 yellow dc, 5 white dc*, 1 yellow dc.
Row 8: Ch 2 to turn, repeat 3 times *7 white dc, 1 yellow dc*, 7 white dc.
Row 9: Ch 2 to turn, repeat 3 times *7 pink dc, 1 gray dc*, 7 pink dc.
Row 10: Ch 2 to turn, 1 gray dc, repeat 3 times *5 pink dc, 3 gray dc*, 5 pink dc, 1 gray dc.
Row 11: Ch 2 to turn, 2 gray dc, repeat 3 times *3 pink dc, 5 gray dc*, 3 pink dc, 2 gray dc.
Row 12: Ch 2 to turn, 3 gray dc, repeat 3 times *1 pink dc, 7 gray dc*, 1 pink dc, 3 gray dc. Cut yarn.

Crochet a second identical piece.

SUPPLIES
· Bergère de France Coton Fifty yarn (#2 fine weight; 4 ply; 50% cotton, 50% acrylic; 153 yd/140 m per 1.8 oz/50 g) in your choice of color
· 3 mm (US C-2 or D-3) hook

STITCHES AND TECHNIQUES
· Magic circle, chain stitch, slip stitch, double crochet: **see Stitches, page 34.**

SUPPLIES
· Bergère de France Coton Fifty yarn (#2 fine weight; 4 ply; 50% cotton, 50% acrylic; 153 yd/140 m per 1.8 oz/50 g) in following colors: Bengale (fuchsia), Turquoise, Coco (white), Cytise (yellow), Berlingot (pink), Perle (gray)
· 3.5 mm (US E-4) hook

FOR MARGUERITE

STITCHES AND TECHNIQUES

• Chain stitch, double crochet: **see Stitches, page 34.**

• Joining with whipstitch: **see Techniques, page 39.**

• Changing colors within a row: Yo, insert hook, yo and pull through the st, yo and pull through 2 loops, yo with new color, pull through last 2 loops with the new color. Example: 3 turquoise dc, 3 pink dc, 3 turquoise dc. In this case, work 3 dc in turquoise (changing colors in the 3rd turquoise dc as explained above), 3 dc in pink (changing colors in the 3rd pink dc), 3 turquoise dc. If the color is different in the 1st dc at the beginning of the row, the color must be changed in the last st of the previous row.

• Do not cut yarn when changing colors, but carry non-working yarn along and work sts over and encircling it so it is hidden, and then the 2 yarns are easily switched when changing colors.

Note: Replace the 1st dc with ch 3.
The 2 ch sts at beginning of the row are a turning ch.

FINISHING

Sew the 2 pieces together with whipstitch, joining Row 12 to Row 12.

Cut 12 strands of yarn about 4 in/10 cm long, and attach 1 fringe made with 3 strands in each corner.